JAMES A.
MICHENER
ON THE SOCIAL STUDIES

National Council for the Social Studies

ISBN 0-87986-060-X
Copyright © 1991 by
NATIONAL COUNCIL FOR THE SOCIAL STUDIES
3501 Newark Street N.W.
Washington, D.C. 20016-3167

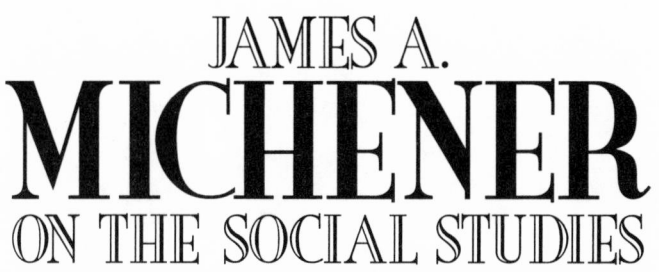

JAMES A. MICHENER ON THE SOCIAL STUDIES

Table of Contents

Preface v

Michener's Early Work: The Foundation Years ix

Music and the Social Studies 1

Participation in Community Surveys as Social Education 7

The Problem of the Social Studies 29

The Beginning Teacher 37

Discussion in the Schools 77

The P.E.A. Report 81

Teachers in the Community 85

The Mature Social Studies Teacher 91

James Michener Comments on Words and Exploration 101

James A. Michener Comments on "The Anti-Science Epidemic" 105

James A. Michener: Reaffirmations of a Permanent Liberal 111

Books by James A. Michener 119

Preface

When the Board of Directors of NCSS selected James A. Michener to be honored for a lifetime of contributions to social education, at the suggestion of Jan Tucker of Florida International University and Program Chair on the Caribbean Conference, discussion centered on appropriate ways to celebrate the event. These ranged from presenting the usual plaques, and certificates, to medals, yet such awards would tell little about his accomplishments. Ironically, the answer should have been apparent from the start. Although the public knows James A. Michener as a prolific writer of well-received fiction and nonfiction, his pre-literary life is that of a writer of salient works published in NCSS's journals and other prominent educational publications. The educational record even overlaps the public Michener the world knows.

To honor him we have gathered copies of his educational writings in NCSS publications, spanning almost 50 years—1938-1987—in a single volume. This is a fitting tribute and a memento to James A. Michener for incisive, insightful, and lasting contributions to our profession.*

While reading and re-reading Mr. Michener's work to prepare this volume, I was struck by his vision for the social studies. It began early in his career and has flourished ever since.

An unintended benefit emerged from the effort of tracing the locations of the various NCSS journals as well as their provenances within the organization. The 1958 doctoral dissertation of Louis Michael Vanaria, *The National Council for the Social Studies: A Voluntary Organization for Professional Service* (Unpublished, Columbia University), proved to be a veritable mine of information revealing some intriguing aspects of the history of the NCSS publication program. For example, the December 1922 issue of *Historical Outlook* became the first yearbook of the Council. Members could receive it by paying one dollar a year. Bulletin #1: *Historical Fiction Suitable for Junior and Senior High Schools* by Hannah Logasa appeared in 1927. By 1931 the arrangement with *Historical Outlook* seemed unsatisfactory and was replaced by *The 1931 Yearbook*, the first publication of

---

* John Kings, Mr. Michener's long-time editorial assistant, gave us strong and enthusiastic encouragement for producing this volume and provided a complete list of Mr. Michener's published works and the photograph of Mr. Michener on the title page. The chronological listing of Mr. Michener's works on education, compiled by Cleta Galvez and John Marshall (*Social Education*, April/May, 1987:274), proved invaluable for tracing copies of his work in NCSS library holdings, NCSS Archives at Teachers College, Columbia University, and in the University of Maryland Library with the assistance of Dr. Joseph Cirrincione of the University's Geography and Education Departments.

this type to be published by the Council. Each yearbook dealt with a single theme on some aspect of teaching social studies including the school structures and environments within which they were taught. By 1934 *Historical Outlook* became *The Social Studies* and *Social Education* was inaugurated in 1937.

The works we decided to include in this volume contain landmark statements in the history of the social studies and American education. All have been selected from *The Social Studies,* Yearbooks of NCSS, and *Social Education*—all "official publications" of the Council.

We expanded the list of Mr. Michener's published works to include two short articles based on his speeches but reprinted or excerpted in *Social Education* as well as an interview by Cleta Galvez (*Social Education*, April/May 1987: 250-255) whose doctoral dissertation, *James A. Michener: Educator* (University of Texas 1984), elaborated on salient aspects of his life as an educator. Dr. Galvez also graciously agreed to write an introduction on her personal reflections of working with Mr. Michener during this period and allowed us to use photographs from her personal collection.

The body of work reproduced in this volume is a vital chronicle of the professional development and writing of James A. Michener. His writings on education reveal an uncanny prescience as well as a thorough grasp of the core problems that surface periodically to confront our profession. The careful reader will uncover the remarkable clarity, breadth, and depth in his writing, his unusual perceptions,

creative thinking, command of an amazing array of literature, and a vast and perceptive knowledge of issues and trends in education and the social studies.

Organization of this Volume

A page containing some significant quotations from the work reproduced precedes each article. I have selected some that reveal his genius at writing a topic sentence while teasing the reader to continue reading. I have chosen some quotations intentionally to tempt the reader rather than reveal at once the nature of the argument or the manner in which he will develop his discourse on a subject. Throughout these works we see Mr. Michener not only as a writer of books but also as a prodigious consumer of them.

* * *

Michener's life resides in the world of books—a serious world where knowledge reposes, aroused only by the inquisitive and probing mind. This diverse world of books, this feast for the penetrating mind, is a treasured gift to be treated with the utmost care. According to Francis Bacon's counsel:

> Some books are to be tasted, others to be swallowed, and some few to be chewed and digested; that is, some books are to be read only in parts; others to be read but cursorily and some to be read wholly, and with diligence and attention. (From the essay, *Of Studies* 1625.)

None of Bacon's advice tells us to avoid them.

This celebration of Michener's social studies writing should invite readers to chew and digest the amazing range of his work from *Tales of the South Pacific* (1947), *Report of the County Chairman*

(1961), *The Source* (1965), *Iberia* (1968), *Kent State* (1971), *Sports in America* (1976), a series of art books published between 1954 and 1970, to *Pilgrimage* (1990), *The Eagle and the Raven* (1990), and *The Novel* (1991). Their scope and substance are lasting testaments to a social studies teacher who speaks to a global audience with confidence.

It is with great pride that we present this volume to James A. Michener on the occasion of the International Social Studies Conference held in Miami, Florida on "The Caribbean: Cradle, Crossroads, and Crucible of the Americas," a region so well chronicled in his book, *Caribbean*. On the occasion of this presentation we also will announce the establishment of the James A. Michener Prize that NCSS will award every five years to an individual whose body of work contributes significantly to the social studies.

James A. Michener has proved himself an instructive and versatile travel companion, trenchant commentator on the American scene, chronicler of minor and major civilizations, and social studies teacher nonpareil. Emily Dickinson's exultant hymn to books embraces our thanks for his guidance, companionship, and voyages:

There is no frigate like a book
To take us lands away
Nor any coursers like a page
Of prancing poetry.

This traverse may the poorest take
Without oppress of toll;
How fragile is the chariot
That bears a human soul!

—Salvatore J. Natoli
Director of Publications and Editor,
Social Education
National Council for the Social Studies
Washington, D.C.

Michener's Early Work: The Foundation Years

Coming to work with
James A. Michener

The National Council for the Social Studies' sponsorship of a conference on the Caribbean has caused me to reflect upon the first time I met James Michener. In the summer of 1983, we were at the University of Texas at Austin: I was studying in the Schools of Education and Business, he was writing his much acclaimed *Texas.* Deliberating dissertation topics on everything from the experience of Alaskan school children to inter- or intra-group behavior in work settings, I simply could not get excited about research on, what appeared to me, mundane subjects (though others could and have!).

Michener during his Hill School years, 1929-1931

Hill School Bulletin, 1981

Michener's presence at the University— a presence all Austinites, especially UT students were acutely aware of— sparked an idea for a dissertation, which frankly I thought to be a long shot. Michener, possibly the most unusual and arguably the most effective educator of our time had a seemingly unexplained past—at least before 1947, the year in which *South Pacific* was published. I started my investigation of these years at Texas and soon thereafter found myself at Harvard University, Columbia University, and Swarthmore College. The archives at Columbia were a virtual gold mine of information on the author's early years. With my East Coast exploration behind me, I returned to Texas and proposed a dissertation topic to my major professor, O. L. Davis. The focus of the dissertation was to explore Michener's early years of writing and teaching as a foundation for understanding the author of later years. The idea was approved, on the condition that I would have access to Michener himself.

After an initial screening, I met Michener and his long-term editorial assistant John Kings in July. Michener interviewed me, asking multiple questions about my background and then suddenly paused, "You know I'm not excited about Ph.D. students who take ten years to complete a dissertation!" Of course not—in later years he would state he wrote ten books in four years. Even in July of 1983, I understood Michener's productivity and that I would have to maintain a healthy pace to work with him. Besides, I was tired of being an impoverished student and wanted to graduate and land a real job. We drew up a pact on that day—I had one year to complete the dissertation and would be granted six or seven lengthy interviews.

Why was I so fortunate to have had the unique opportunity to work with such a renowned author? Little doubt I was in the right place, at the right time, with what I think was the right dissertation topic. Provided that as a truism, I believe Michener also has an affinity for young people. While I was conducting biographical research, Jesus de la Tejá and Robert Wooster were assisting Michener as he collected data for *Texas*. Dr. Tejá would later work for the Texas General Land Office; Dr. Wooster would later teach history at Corpus Christi State University. At the same time Michener was working with Ph.D. candidates, he had two excellent support people working for him—Lisa Kaufman and Debbie Brothers. Lisa, a Wesleyan graduate, is now an editor for the Viking Penguin Press and Debbie Brothers recently published Michener's own work—*The Eagle and the Raven* (1990). Michener had many young people working for him, I was just one more. I cannot speak for the other students, but for me, he would affect my learning, my writing and though he did not know it, acted as a role model for my future work.

Michener, A Familiar Teacher

People know James Michener. His novels line the bookstands in airports, most book stores, and numerous other stores that may carry books only as a sideline. Published in fifty-two languages, his books have been made into twelve movies and an equal number of television specials. To this day, Michener is discussed in corporate lunchrooms, boutiques, and on commuter trains. An American Christmas tradition has become a gift of a book written by Michener. This author maintains a fantastic sensitive antenna for what is happening in the world and consequently escorts his readers out of their classrooms, factories, and offices to experience other cultures, geographies, religions, and attitudes. Michener, whose career progressed from high school teaching, to university teaching, to textbook publishing, and now to writing has persistently remained loyal to a social studies curriculum. From scholar to storyteller, he claims his subject remains the same, only his audience has changed (Michener 1970, 76):

> I think of my books as an extension of my early commitments; creative teaching expressed in a different way. Certainly my concern with social studies, geography, politics, economics, cultural history, current social problems has never diminished and I have tried in general to keep abreast of new developments in these fields. One might say I was dismissed as a professor but retained as a teacher.

Early Commitments to Learning and Teaching

Michener's early commitments to learning and teaching are clear as one reflects on his biography. His career, however, was one without a fixed course, aim or goal. Insatiably curious, earnest, and hard-working, Michener's profession evolved by following his interests, intuitions and seizing the momentous vicissitudes of his time. Graduating from Swarthmore College

Alumni Chapel, The Hill School. Courtesy the author.

on the eve of the depression, Michener landed his first job at The Hill School in the fall of 1929. The Hill, a prestigious, private, all-male institution in Pottstown, Pennsylvania became his home as a beginning English teacher. A master in residence, Michener was drawn to a fellow Quaker and colleague—the visionary John Lester. Through his association with Lester, Michener first became exposed to the ideals of the Progressive Education Movement that would influence the next decade of his life.

As a beginning teacher, Michener would read voraciously as he served hall duty six nights a week, from 8:30 to 11:00 P.M. He also formed the habit of spending long hours playing his phonograph records (on a fourth-hand victrola) softly, so he could learn the great operas. The music of Caruso, Martinelli, Rethberg, and Tetrazzini enriched his life and education. To this day, Michener's passion for music continues. He states (1990, 30-31):

Each day, without fail, I find time to listen to music on my new compact disc player, a marvel of these times, with cartridges into which I can load six of the miraculous silver circles, each giving an hour of almost perfect sound reproduction. Into one cartridge I place the piano music of Chopin, Beethoven, and Liszt. In another, six of my perennial favorites: the Schubert *Octet*, the Bartok *Concerto for Orchestra*, the Brahms *First*, the Beethoven *Ninth*, the Stravinsky *Rite of Spring* and *Petrouchka*. In a third, six wonderful discs of the great operatic arias, some by Caruso and his peers in the 1920s, some by the current stars.

Possibly Michener considers music essential to his continuous work performance. He claims, "music is perhaps the finest single instrument we have by which to achieve the development of fine, sensitive imaginations" (Michener 1938, 43).

Two years after becoming a teacher (in 1931), somewhat stifled by the stringent regime and milieu of The Hill School, Michener resigned his position to accept the Lippincott Fellowship awarded him by Swarthmore College. He commenced his first overseas adventure to study at the University of St. Andrews in Scotland and the University of Siena in Italy. The globalization of Michener's perspectives began herein and enjoyed continuous maturation throughout his career.

While still in Europe, headmaster George Walton contacted Michener to recruit him to teach English at The George School, a Quaker, co-educational, progressive institution in southeastern Pennsylvania. In 1933, he accepted the position and upon his return to the states, became involved in the progressive education movement. The movement was then part of a larger sociopolitical movement of general reform blooming in American life during the late 19th and early 20th centuries. It was then that Woodrow Wilson curbed powerful trusts and monopolies to ensure a system of political democracy; Jane Adams worked in a Chicago settlement house and championed the notion that the underprivileged had much to contribute to the spiritual life of the community; and Franklin D. Roosevelt promised a "New Deal" to a nation mired in economic disarray. This general movement to reform American life and institutions changed significantly the essence of America. Its effects on education and Michener himself were not inconsequential.

Michener's experience working at The George School allowed him to participate in the Progressive Education Association's "eight year study." The author described the George

School at that time, "We tended to be socially conservative but intellectually we were at the cutting edge, we were that movement (Galvez 1984, 13)." It was also during these socially seductive years that Michener made a deliberate and conscious shift to teaching social studies.

Continuous involvement with the eight-year study provided Michener with yet another opportunity—a summer with Ralph Tyler and Boyd Bode at Ohio State University, where his interests were again redirected—this time to the more progressive laboratory school. In the fall of 1937, he left the George School to assume a position at the Colorado State College of Education at Greeley (known today as the University of Northern Colorado at Greeley). Far more experimental than the George School, College High School focused on assisting undergraduate students to teach. These were important years for Michener as he taught, engaged in his M.A. in secondary education, and began a steady output of educational literature, many of which were topics on timely teaching activities. Unintentionally, he attracted great attention because of the geography of the school's locale. He explained (Galvez 1984, 5):

> ...when any committee was put together you'd have somebody from Harvard, Yale, Princeton, North Carolina and then maybe Pittsburgh and Michigan and the...West Coast. Then there was this guy in the middle...I got more attention there than I would have had I gone to Yale because I was the only person for 2,000 miles.

It was during these Colorado years that Michener developed a deep con-

(l-r) James A. Michener, Cleta Galvez, Wilbur Murra, 1985. Courtesy the author.

cern for public education. Having completed an M.A., he now turned his attention to doctoral study.

In 1939, Michener became actively involved in the NCSS Publications Committee and in 1940 became its chair. Wilbur Murra, a long time colleague, assumed the first, full-time, paid position of NCSS as Executive Secretary at the same time. As chair of the committee, Michener arranged for publication of contemporary social studies topics and contributed his own manuscripts for NCSS publications while developing his writing skills.

Approximately the same time Michener was appointed to the NCSS Publications Committee, he received a teaching appointment with Howard Wilson at The Harvard University Graduate School of Education. As Senior Lecturer, he taught a traditional methods course and an experimental course sponsored by the Progressive Education Association. Simultaneously, he pursued his own education, wrote, and edited manuscripts for NCSS. Michener left, possibly his most stimulating environment to date,

to return to Greeley as an Associate Professor. With increased academic responsibilities at Colorado, he reached an impasse in his career.

Although he had completed the course work for the Ed.D. at Harvard, the times required professors in his position to have a Ph.D. in a subject area. Since Michener did not have knowledge of the two required classical languages, German or French, he understood that a Ph.D. would not be easy to obtain. A lucrative offer from Macmillan Publishing Company in 1941, thus enticed Michener from academia to the world of textbook publishing. In reflecting on his break with academia, he said (Galvez 1984, 3):

> I wasn't bitter about it but I sure was aware of it...I had used up academia and academia was not going to have much to offer me...everybody wanted me but I was not going to get a tenured professorship anywhere.

Less than two years after accepting the Macmillan appointment, however, Michener enlisted in the Navy and was plunged into the war in the South Pacific. The rest is history. Today, however, Michener returns to the university environments, in which he finds solace and to which he passionately responds.

Michener's Early Work: A Window for the Future

Under the rubric of the social studies, Michener promoted that which he intensely believed in—life experience education and the experimental social studies curriculum. Recurrent themes will emerge as one examines the subsequent works contained herein—idealism in education, the importance of social consciousness, devotion to progressive education, and so on. Not surprisingly, Michener attracted people far and wide during these early publishing years as he emanated energy and enthusiasm while fostering new ideas.

As I write this preface, the war in the Persian Gulf region has just ended. The parallels of motives for the U.S. entry into Operation Desert Storm do not appear greatly dissimilar with those Michener described in "What Are We Fighting For?" (1941). Michener noted then, that America was "creeping" into a war when much of her population maintained no clear conception about its lessons for fighting. He identified reasons for America's involvement in the war and offered suggestions for enhancing the concept of democracy in the classroom. Are there not lessons to revisit in this article?

As we mentioned earlier, Michener has always had a fantastic sensitive antenna. As you peruse these manuscripts, reflect not just on early times, but our own times—our own seductive histories—and ponder the lessons of this fine teacher.

References

Galvez, Cleta M. "James Michener: Oral History No. 3." 1984. Files of Cleta Galvez, Minneapolis-St. Paul.

Michener, James A. "Bach and Sugar Beets." *Music Educators Journal*, Volume 30 (September 1938): 29 and 43.

Michener, James A. "What are We Fighting For?" *Progressive Education*, Volume 18 No. 7. (1941): 342-348.

Michener, James A. "The Mature Social Studies Teacher." *Social Education*, Volume 34 (November 1970): 760-767.

Michener, James A. *The Eagle and The Raven.* Texas: State House Press, 1990.

Cleta M. Galvez is a member of the Executive Resources Department at 3M in St.Paul, Minnesota. She currently leads the Organizational Planning and Control Committee of the Women's Advisory Council at 3M.

Dr. Galvez's career includes experience in academia and business. Prior to joining 3M, Cleta assisted in establishing executive development programs for American Airlines in Dallas, Texas, and worked on a technical management project for Tracor, Inc., Austin, Texas. At the University of Texas at Austin, she worked as a research associate for a national research and development center.

Cleta Galvez received her Ph.D. in 1984 from The University of Texas at Austin, having studied in both the graduate schools of education and business administration. She received the Distinguished Dissertation Award from Kappa Delta Pi after having worked with James A. Michener and his associates on a biography of the first 40 years of his life. She also received a Fulbright Scholarship in 1978 to study in India. She holds a B.A. from Siena College in Loudonville, New York.

JAMES A. MICHENER
ON THE SOCIAL STUDIES

Music and the Social Studies

in
The Social Studies
Volume XXVIII, Number 1
January 1937
Pages 28-30

66 [Music can be put to two fundamental uses] in so far as it relates to history. The first of these occurs when the music is merely illustrative cultural material that will assist the student in obtaining a picture of some definite geographical entity, or some definite historical period of man's development. …[E]ach country has its own peculiar forms of music—forms which will contribute to making that country real. There is in music, something elemental, something belonging definitely to place and national culture.

The second fundamental way in which music may be used is less easily administered, but I think, much more valuable than the merely illustrative use that I have been discussing. Music is a very powerful assistant in discussing deep-rooted social problems. 99

Music and the Social Studies

JAMES A. MICHENER

*Director of the Social Studies, The Secondary School, Colorado State
College of Education, Greeley, Colorado*

There are two situations in which music may be used to great advantage in the field of the social studies. The first occurs when the teacher of the social studies is also interested in music. He will find rising naturally to his attention forms of musical art that will supplement his teaching and enrich it in many unique ways. The second, and more common situation develops when the teacher of social studies is himself only slightly acquainted with music, but is willing to turn over some of his class time to an enthusiastic and inventive music teacher.

I have worked in both situations, and I do not think that either has a great advantage over the other. The more satisfying correlation of materials probably comes when one teacher administers both the music and the social studies; but the educational experience for the child is probably more significant when another teacher enters the classroom with a new field of thought at his command, thus illustrating clearly that all subjects are related. In whichever situation a teacher may find himself, he can rest assured that there are great possibilities inherent in the use of music in many of his classes.

When one uses this art-form for long, he finds that there are two fundamental uses to which it can be put, in so far as it relates to the study of history. The first of these occurs when the music is merely illustrative cultural material that will assist the student in obtaining a picture of some definite geographical entity, or some definite historical period of man's development. This is, of course, the basic use of music in the field of the social studies. In studying Russia, for example, I have always tried to use Moussorgsky's "Pictures at an Exhibition," excerpts from "Boris Godounov," and "A Night on the Bare Mountain." Rimsky-Korsakoff's "Russian Easter" is almost perfect as an illustrative work describing sociological conditions in Russia. Similarly, Borodin's "On the Steppes of Central Asia" will give a view of the great sweep of Russian peasant life, and Tschaikowsky's sure-fire "1812 Overture" and "Marche Slav" will always be enjoyed by students of high school age.

Thus each country has its own peculiar forms of music—forms which will contribute to making that country real. There is in music, something elemental, something belonging definitely to place and national culture. Sibelius, Brahms, Cesar Franck, Smetana,

Ferdie Grofe, Delius, Strauss, and de Falla are all perfect examples of composers whose works bear indelibly the stamp of their nation. I sometimes feel that it is more important for students to meet with these men than with another book on a foreign country. I have found that the students with whom I come in contact are able to comprehend the most delicate colors of this type of music. At first I limited myself to excerpts impossible of failure, such as the works of Strauss and Tschaikowsky. I had been teaching something of the geography of Italy preparatory to a unit on the unification. I discovered that more than half of the class did not know the difference between Venice and Vienna. I happened to have at hand Strauss' "The Artist's Life" which I played for the group. Then we heard "Tale from a Vienna Woods." Finally a girl discovered the similarity between this work and the "Blue Danube," and with that as a basis, we proceeded to fix firmly the difference between the two cities, each of which was to be important in the next few weeks.

After class several students conveyed their appreciation of this type of illustrative material. As a result I was encouraged to use more of it, and with the help of the music teacher, I was able to find materials for most of the countries we dealt with. After that experience, I have almost come to the conclusion that it is foolish to try to give students any idea of what the Baltic provinces are like if one does not use the music of Sibelius. As soon as a teacher admits to himself that one of his foremost objectives in dealing with Europe is to convey to the student a tangible feeling for the widely varied types of life existing there, then he is almost obligated to spend some of his classroom time with the music of Europe.

Similarly, much of the world's greatest music typifies precise periods of man's historical development. A large percentage of the operas deal with the cultural periods most often taught in high schools. If teachers in progressive schools are serious in their attempts to give students the best of a few periods rather than everything of all the periods, then the great field of story-music should be used in the classroom. The first indication I received of the richness of this field came when some students told me that "The Sorcerer's Apprentice" was a story about science in the Middle Ages. A splendid music teacher had seen fit to tell them this, hoping that it would be of value to them in other classes. "Till Eulenspiegel" is an even better story of the Middle Ages, and as we later learned, "Faust" is not merely a picture of the Middle Ages—it is that period. Yet for years we have tried to inculcate into the teaching of our history some vague idea of what the period was like, and at the same time we have failed to use "Parsifal," "Lohengrin," "Tristan und Isolde," and "William Tell."

Today, however, these operas are being broadcast by radio throughout the year, and teachers can direct their students to these perfect examples of historical documents. In many of the progressive schools excerpts or even entire operas are available. These can well be used once in two weeks as a welcome break in classroom routine. Their instructional value is very high.

In the same way almost every period that one wishes to study has some opera or some bit of program music that students can understand and enjoy. The period of the Renaissance is amply covered by such works as "Rigoletto," "Boris Godounov," "Falstaff," "Lucia di Lammermoor," and "Il Trovatore." I have used excerpts from these operas from time to time, and have found them quite useful in building up a feeling for the period under discussion. In the modern period one may use Stravinsky's easier works, good orchestrations by Paul Whiteman, some torrid music by our colored bands, and rich swing music of the moderns. There is no reason why music, which is certainly a profound part of any national or cultural development, should be ignored in social studies.

The second fundamental way in which music may be used is less easily administered but, I think, much more valuable than the merely illustrative use that I have just been discussing. Music is a very powerful assistant in discussing deep-rooted social problems. It is in this field, I believe, that the best work will be done in the next few years as far as the interrelation of music and the social studies is concerned. Many of the most trying modern problems can be illustrated by forms of music. In dealing with the question of economic repression we should use the great songs of the negro, or the folk songs of the north countries, or the sentimental ballads of the mountaineer. Repression has called these things forth, and they are part of the human experience, oftentimes the most poignant part. War, invasion, tyranny, urban versus rural life, the machine age, the jazz age, the problems of religion—all these things can be marvelously illustrated with music, ranging from the very greatest opera down to the current sob-ballad that will last a month at the most.

Another method of using music as sociological material consists of playing unnamed phonograph records to the class, telling the students only that the

composer, like all great men, was deeply worried about some fundamental social problem when he wrote this music. The students are to listen attentively as the music is played three or four times; then they are to express in either simple or imaginative prose the conflicts that have been presented in this music. I have experimented with this type of work for the past two years. I have used classes of the tenth, eleventh, and twelfth levels, students both advanced and retarded, both enthusiastic and suspicious. The results have been much finer than I had any right to expect. I have always turned the papers over either to the music teacher, another social studies teacher or an English teacher for comment, and each of these participants in the experiment has expressed surprise at the maturity of expression.

I am careful to choose music of a dramatic nature. It is best to start with vocal music. Verdi's works are splendid if care is taken in selecting passages that are not too confused. Verdi tends to utilize basic emotional problems, so that a student with an average imagination can sense the struggle developing between the individuals. Parts of the works of Wagner, particularly the mystical selections, are fine for this type of work. Arrigo Boito has supplied several selections that have been most productive. The older spirituals have sometimes surpassed even Verdi and Wagner in the excellence of the responses they have called forth.

In time it is easy to introduce purely orchestral music, if care is taken in seeing that it is dramatic and expressive. The best selection I have ever used in this type of work is Borodin's "On the Steppes of Central Asia." The responses were so vigorous, so attuned to the music that I wondered if the children could have been informed of its contents before I presented the music to them.

In administering musical excerpts dealing with social problems the teacher will have to decide how much suggestion he will give his students. After three or four times I offer no explanatory remarks. Occasionally it is profitable to say that the music is Russian, or Spanish. Sometimes I have identified the voices they are to hear. At other times I explain when the music was written, but for the most part these introductions are unnecessary. In all of this experimenting I have had to revise my opinions of adolescent ability. There seems to be no limit beyond which the youthful mind cannot project itself when inspired by magnificent thoughts. Time and again half the class has hit upon the precise idea held by the composer when he wrote. I have found that when a student, sitting in a classroom, listening to something he has never heard before, suddenly realizes that he is listening to the presentation of a terrible conclusion to a battle, the discovery in some way electrifies him into identifying himself with the misery and the shame of war. Time and again I have had boys and girls tell me, long after a unit was completed, that they remembered the music as the best part of the whole study.

When introducing music into the social studies there are two ways of administering it: the social studies teacher may select and present the music, or the teacher of music may be called in to discuss and present the program. Music may be used in two ways: as illustrative cultural material or as psychological and sociological material. In the first use, the music refers principally to countries or to his-torical periods. In the second use, the music may be administered either as a definite expression of some deep-rooted problem, or as an unidentified ex-pression which the students themselves are to identify in simple or imaginative prose. The principal value of music so used is that the student is invited, often times impelled, to project himself into foreign countries, past ages, or gripping situations. Music has this power of inviting self-projection because it is, above all else, one expression of the finest thought of any country or any period.

JAMES A.
MICHENER
ON THE SOCIAL STUDIES

Participation in Community Surveys as Social Education

in

Utilization of Community Resources in the Social Studies
1938 Yearbook
Ruth West, Editor
National Council for the Social Studies
pages 144-163

> " Today American education professes to train all young people, not primarily for the professions, but for citizenship in a democracy. ...Today schools are the first organized bulwark of democracy with which the young child comes in contact.
>
> [Selecting community problems for study requires four criteria:] First, the survey must deal with a problem within the realm of student interest. ...[Second,] Will our study of this problem be of service to the community when finished? ...[Third,] Does the proposed project have a discoverable body of fact upon which the pupils will be able to formulate sound generalizations? ...[Fourth, we should be able to] confine our activity to those surveys which the community itself has asked for. "

PARTICIPATION IN COMMUNITY SURVEYS AS SOCIAL EDUCATION

James A. Michener

As American national life has matured, new functions have been allotted to the schools. Education was once the training of a few young men who were intended for the learned professions. Today American education professes to train all young people, not primarily for the professions, but for citizenship in a democracy. Schools were once appendages of a paternalistic colonial system, and as such had carefully prescribed functions to fulfill. Today schools are the first organized bulwark of democracy with which the young child comes into contact. When the American school recognizes and accepts these implications, changes will have to be made in the curriculum. The whole field of citizenship education must be reconsidered in the light of the new functions of the school.

New Techniques in Citizenship Education

Citizenship education has been directed at the understanding of some nebulous government in Washington. Few children have been able to comprehend it fully, exemplifying once more the national fallacy of training a few at the expense of the many. We have not only directed our civics teaching at the upper twenty-five per cent of our students, but also at a remote government; while all the time there have been in the community real-life citizenship problems which any student could understand. For expediency and applicability, if for no other reason, social education dealing with community problems can be justified.

The nature of the school's participation in these problems can be represented by answers to three questions. (1) What problems are recommended for school study? (2) How should these problems be studied? (3) How should they be reported to the community? Any intelligent educator knows what the school should *not* do in community participation. Schools should not sponsor one candidate over another in either a national or local election. Public schools probably should not officially lobby for specific legislation. They should not attempt to stigmatize any segment of the population, and they have no right to anathematize individuals.

Schools do, however, have a right to analyse all party platforms and the credentials of all candidates. Many educators would say such analysis is a major obligation of the curriculum. Schools certainly should dissect projected legislation, realizing that their technique and findings may influence the parents of their students. In local affairs, the school must recognize many social problems. Housing, health, working conditions, safety, vocational opportunities, recreational opportunities, local social services, law enforcement, bond issues, and projected amendments to state constitutions are all problems which the school can study.

After a problem has been identified for study, the question of how to attack it is of next importance. There appear to be four prevailing methods. (1) The teacher can discuss the problem with the pupils, bringing out their prejudices, doing his best to counteract them, and indirectly imposing his own particular prejudices. This weak method warrants the title "Indoctrination." Any study of primary sources has been done by one man—the teacher; and the results are naturally influenced by one man's preconceptions and misconceptions. (2) The teacher can discuss the problem with his students and direct them to reading material which they can utilize in an effort to discover for themselves generalizations which they can reasonably defend. Most American teachers appear to be dissatisfied with anything less than this method. It probably represents the minimum essential in teaching community problems. (3) The third method is similar to the second but adds to it class excursions in which teacher and students visit the locale of the problem being studied. Speakers can often bring the scene of the problem to the classroom. Visual and auditory aids may be introduced, always for the purpose of making the problem a life situation which the students can understand. This method of teaching is probably appropriate for most American schools and can be recommended where classes are large and teacher time filled with many non-instructional tasks. (4) The most satisfactory way of studying local problems is by the problem-solving method. Students and teacher, working together, establish problems to be studied, as for example, "How Can Traffic Accidents in Greeley Be Controlled?" Pertinent reading material is utilized, but if satisfactory information is to be acquired the techniques of the community survey become essential. Field trips, interviews, traffic counts, questionnaires, the construction of graphs, and the making of reports assume primary importance. These activities provide the principal sources of data

10

upon which the students base their concluding generalizations. This method in its entirety is properly termed "The Survey Method."

The inherent nature of this educational procedure demands that something shall be done with the findings of the completed study. There are two standard procedures in reporting results. Students who make the survey may discuss their findings with other students in the school, thus creating a whole-school attitude upon the question. Many secondary school community surveys like those on favorite recreation, movie habits, or occupational opportunities should terminate in this manner, for their subjects pertain directly to problems which the students themselves can solve. There are other problems like housing, law enforcement, and legislation which deserve community consideration. Any surveys of these problems should be reported to the community through the newspaper, radio, or public forum.

If appropriate local problems are studied according to the best methods and reported to the community attractively, laudable outcomes for students, community, and school should result. (1) The school has the right to anticipate that its pupils will develop into better citizens. (2) They will be more intelligent concerning the nature of community life. (3) They will be able to study other local problems for themselves and arrive at justifiable conclusions. (4) When they become adult voters, they should be more concerned about local government and social improvement than most adults now are. Finally, pupils gain a confidence in their own powers and in their own personalities. Many schools that sponsor problem surveys terminating in public reports to the community find that their pupils improve noticeably in each of the four areas of development listed above.

The school which conducts appropriate surveys also has a right to anticipate improved relations between itself and the community. If in making the surveys the creation of needless animosities is avoided, many communities will not only approve but sponsor such activity. There is abundant testimony that when the schools cooperate for the social welfare of the people, the people will support the schools.

The school also has a right to anticipate the gradual enrichment of community life if pupils study actual community situations. In the first place, a more cooperative citizenry will lead to a more cooperative community. If the schools can educate pupils in the attributes of social intelligence, political astuteness, reasoning, and confidence in the democratic procedures, the life of each individual and city will reflect such training. Over many years the national level of intelligent citizenship may be raised and education will share in the results. In the second place, any community with a vigorous school should be able to see immediate results of that school's program. Playground facilities may be increased and juvenile delinquency decreased; traffic problems may be simplified; the use of harmful drugs may be reduced; housing conditions may be improved; and the lot of the underprivileged may be ameliorated. Such tangible results have been achieved in many American communities within the last ten years.

Four Criteria for Selecting Community Problems for Study

Many phases of community life are worthy of careful study by the school. Teachers and administrators need some basis upon which to select potentially excellent surveys and upon which to reject others which will prove to be of little value. The Secondary School of Colorado State College of Education chooses problems for survey according to four criteria. First, *the survey must deal with a problem within the realm of student interest.* This criterion does not disbar many studies, for student interest in community problems is most catholic. Safety and recreation, however, would probably contribute more to a solution of adolescent problems than would a factual study of tenure of county office holders or government regulation of inter-state vegetable trucking. Our school has tried to center its attention upon problems in which the students are immediately interested, and secondly upon problems which the majority of adults will face in any community in which they may live. In this way the community survey can contribute to sound social education.

The second criterion is the utility of the problem. *Will our study of this problem be of service to the community when finished?* Such surveys as "Air Traffic in the West," "The Decline of Silver Mining in Colorado," and "The Covered Bridges of Bucks County" represent excellent studies for individual groups, but they can hardly be said to contribute noticeably to the welfare of the community. Whenever possible we prefer our surveys to combine pupil interest and community usefulness. Such studies might be "Should Greeley, Colorado, Have a Federal Housing Project?" "Should Our Town Build a Playground?" "What Will Be the Effect of Amendment Three upon Taxation?" With care, such projects can always be found.

The third criterion is most important. *Does the proposed project have a discoverable body of fact upon which the pupils will be able to formulate sound generalizations?* Some very interesting community problems remain largely in the field of opinion and do not admit of factual treatment by high-school children. On the other hand, involved questions of engineering, sanitation, and road building, in which more than half the data is abstrusely mathematical, should probably be avoided. One of the major objectives of the community survey is to encourage each student to solve his problems in accordance with known facts. Teachers must therefore, before they launch the survey, be certain that data relevant to the problem is available and intelligible to students.

The Secondary School of the College of Education has now reached the stage in its development of citizenship training in which it can introduce for its purposes a fourth criterion not yet applicable to all schools. We have conducted so many successful surveys that *we can now confine our activity to those surveys which the community itself has asked for*. We may choose from the surveys requested those which satisfy the other three criteria; we no longer have to search for a situation in which we can make a public presentation of our findings. When our school launches a survey commissioned by the community, a public hearing has already been arranged for.

Thirteen Typical Surveys

The chart which follows illustrates the significant features of community surveys in our school over a two-year period. In that time five out of thirteen surveys were conducted at the request of the community. Eight of the thirteen were or will be reported to the public. Five were principally concerned with problems in which the students were interested, but in which little or no adult interest had been expressed. Two of these, *Recreation* and *Business Opportunities,* were among the most interesting and well received, so that a school might be unwise to stress community demand too strongly. We try to establish a reasonable balance between community demand and pupil interest. Occasionally a problem stresses one to the exclusion of the other. If the community requests a survey which is uninteresting to pupils and of limited importance, it is not undertaken. If the survey is *apparently* uninteresting to pupils but important to the community, the pupils are invited to volunteer to do some good work for their city. The school has never failed to obtain enough students for such surveys, and the pupils themselves have with one exception enjoyed the work after the first week.

Title	Grades	No. of Students	Weeks	Student request	Teacher request	Community request	Public presentation	School presentation	Class presentation	Value to Other Classes	Cost
School Legislation	11–12	14	8			x		x	x		—
Traffic Survey	7– 8	18	5	x	x		x	x	x	x	$ 0.80
Beet Sugar Industry	10–11	11	11		x			x	x		$4.48
Housing Survey	8– 9	13	8		x		x	x	x	x	$1.90
Business Opportunities	11–12	12	10	x				x	x		$2.08
Recreation for Youth	8– 9	12	14	x				x	x		$0.80
Bicycle Survey	11	15	8			x	x	x	x	x	$11.80
Property Protection	8– 9	12	11	x	x			x	x		—
Occupational Survey	7	24		x				x	x	x	$7.50
Working Hours for College Girls	11–12	3		x				x	x		—
Buying Survey	11–12	10	6			x	(To be initiated in Autumn, 1938)				
Available Social Agencies	11–12	10	6	x		x	(To be initiated in Autumn, 1938)				
Medical Care	11–12	10	6			x	(To be initiated in Winter, 1939)				

SCHOOL LEGISLATION

Purpose: to analyse the effect of proposed amendments to the state constitution upon the educational structure of the state.

Proposer: state educational associations; pupils, who were interested in the initiative and referendum system of the state; and the teacher, who was interested in the election generally.

Sources of Data: county tax rolls; assessments for past years; comparative tax levies in various counties; opinions of local political, educational, and civic leaders; daily papers; statements of predicted cuts in school money.

Form of Presenting Conclusions: graphs; essays; plays; mock meetings of city council, the Chamber of Commerce, the real estate board, the Parent-Teachers Associations; school assemblies.

Public Presentations: none, except school-wide assemblies which some parents attended.

Lasting Results: discriminatory legislation was defeated, and all publication of fact must have helped in attaining this end. The school did not campaign against the amendments, for both sides were heard in the gathering of data and in the assemblies.

Unusual Expenses: none.

TRAFFIC SURVEY

Purpose: to examine traffic conditions in Greeley, and to recommend new laws or procedures if the data warranted such recommendations.

Proposer: the class, in conference with two teachers.

Sources of Data: inspection of police records, of traffic accidents in the city for the past two years; traffic counts; interviews with citizens, law enforcing agents, hospital directors, city council; questionnaires to citizens; field trips and surveys.

Form of Presentation: a map of the city streets was drawn in outline form, with notations of the number of traffic accidents occurring at each intersection; speeches were prepared.

Public Presentation: the pupils took their findings to the local Committee on Safety and to the city council, where the charts were explained in detail; the findings were published in the local paper.

Lasting Results: traffic regulations were changed to afford maximum protection at dangerous intersections as discovered by the survey; the city council mimeographed the report and has distributed it widely in civic clubs throughout the city; the findings have been used as instructional material in other courses.

Unusual Expenses: two mimeographed stencils were cut, and two hundred copies of questionnaires were printed, at a total cost of $0.80.

BEET SUGAR INDUSTRY

Purpose: to determine the relationship between the extensive beet sugar industry and local economic, social, and political life.

Proposer: the author, who wished to determine exactly how expensive it was to conduct such a survey when no printed materials were available in the school at the start of the course. Fifty-two of seventy-five pupils to whom the problems were explained requested permission to take the course.

Sources of Data: government bulletins; propaganda for and against the industry; doctoral dissertations from near and distant universities; interviews with representatives of various branches of the industry; field trips; field surveys of public opinion; statistical data from governmental yearbooks and census reports.

Form of Presentation: graphs; essays; novelettes; poems; model farms; panel discussions; debates; notebooks; art work.

Public Presentation: none.

Lasting Results: the creative productions of the pupils such as notebooks, stories, poems; the collection of materials on the beet industry to be used in subsequent studies of the same problem.

Unusual Expenses: postage; automobile expenses for trips; ten copies of an essential pamphlet; materials for constructing the model farm. $4.48.

Housing Survey

Purpose: to gain an understanding of housing problems present in all cities; to compare housing in three contrasting economic sections of the city; to see whether or not some kind of public housing project is possible among the poor people of the city.

Proposer: community groups sponsored principally by the American Association of University Women; students were permitted to elect other classes if this project did not appeal to them.

Sources of Data: field surveys; research studies; extended interviews with social service workers and community nurses; spending a day with a social service worker on the job; house to house interviews.

Form of Presentation: tables, graphs; speeches before a public forum; preparing an article for the local newspaper; taking photographs and making slides from them; essays.

Public Presentation: a town forum was held at which the pupils participating in the survey presented their findings, made recommendations, answered questions from the floor; the meeting and the data were reported in the local paper.

Lasting Results: the findings are being used by students in a lower grade as study material; the city has appointed a committee to investigate housing possibilities.

Unusual Expenses: mimeographing and printing 200 questionnaires; gasoline for trips; cost of slides. $1.90.

Recreation for Youth

Purpose: to encourage the students conducting the survey to spend their leisure time more wisely.

Proposer: students requested that they study this aspect of community life, the larger unit of which it became a part, having been required.

Sources of Data: interviewing local men and women; reports of national recreational committees; questionnaires to students of other schools; field surveys.

Form of Presentation: graphs; tables; panel discussions; short stories; plays; essays; cartoons; notebooks.

Public Presentation: none.

Lasting Results: the findings of this survey have since been used as instructional material in other classes.

Unusual Expenses: mimeographing of questionnaires. $0.80.

Property Protection

Purpose: to determine the extent to which a city provides protection for the property of its citizens; to determine what extra protection a citizen may obtain other than that provided by general taxation.

Proposer: students requested that they study this aspect of community life, the larger unit, of which it was part, having been required.

Sources of Data: secondary sources in school, college, and town library; primary sources from fire departments, police departments, insurance agents, city engineer, city health officer, field surveys; records of fire and police departments.

Form of Presentation: graphs, charts, tables; stories, essays, plays, panel discussions.

Public Presentation: none; except panel discussions before larger school groups.

Unusual Expenses: none.

OCCUPATIONAL SURVEY

Purpose: to acquaint pupils with the various types of work done by the citizens of Greeley; to provide an introduction to the problem of choosing a vocation.

Proposer: pupils requested this survey as a part of the study of Greeley.

Sources of Data: excursion trips to various industries; statistical data from the United States Census Bureau; survey of the occupations of the parents of students in the secondary school.

Form of Presentation: essays and stories of trips; graphic representations; these are to be placed in a class book on Greeley.

Public Presentation: none.

Lasting Results: materials will be used by other pupils and other classes; more intelligent understanding of occupations and vocations should result; material has been tabulated for use by the guidance office.

Unusual Expenses: busses for trips to factories. $7.50.

The last three surveys listed in the table represent results a school should expect to obtain after a year and a half's careful experimentation with community service. The "Buying Survey" has been requested by a group of business men who want to know what they can do to improve their service to local housewives. They present us with a new problem, however, for they wish to bear all the expenses of the survey. The school has decided not to accept this offer, because we want our pupils and our community to feel that schools are in the community to serve it. By not permitting the community to share the expense of our surveys we are also better able to refuse those requests which might represent mere exploitation of the school or its students. The results of this survey are assured wide publication.

The survey of "Available Social Agencies in Greeley" has been requested by a group of public spirited women who are leaders in the social work of the community. They fear that much duplication results from a lack of coordination of the available social agencies. Our pupils will be expected to survey social service work in Greeley, report their findings, and make what recommendations seem practical. These two surveys have been planned in outline form and will be launched at the beginning of the school year. The third projected survey is of a similar nature, but we are as yet uncertain of our ability to conduct it.

Techniques of Instruction Used in Community Surveys

Teachers need not fear that participating in a community survey means a holiday from training in the basic techniques of learning. There are ample opportunities in any survey for review of old skills and the introduction of new. Problem solving is the standard method by which to conduct a survey, and this scientific approach demands that every student use many of the basic learning skills. The steps followed by our students in launching a survey are definite; they have been tested and proved over a period of six years. We find they afford an excellent introduction to the processes of scientific thinking. Students can be taught to master each of the following techniques.

Identifying the problem. The first step in any community activity is the formulation of a problem upon which the students are to work. The class should discuss all aspects of the large area under consideration and agree upon one problem, stated as a question, which conforms to five criteria. (1) It should contain one idea. (2) It should be comprehensive, but not involved. (3) It should not be answerable by a "yes" or "no" reply. (4) It should be unambiguous and pertinent, so that only a portion of all the conceivable data can apply to it. "What About Traffic?" and "What Shall We Do About Safety?" are so vague that even remotely relevant data might apply to their solution. (5) The problem should have some social significance. Students in the Traffic Survey chose as their main problem *How Can Traffic Accidents Be Controlled?*

Analysing the Problem demands that the class break down the main question into contributory ones. The purpose of this step is to simplify the work so that a reasonable approach to the larger problem is possible. The first step in analysing the above problem would be to define the words "traffic," "accidents" and "control." From this step students might decide upon the following subsidiary problems:

What are the kinds of accidents?
What are the causes of traffic accidents in Greeley?
How can each type of accident be controlled?
What can the city do to improve its traffic regulations?

The teacher should probably not dominate the class during the analy-sis; he may well spend his time directing the discussion of the pupils into avenues of thought that promise to be fruitful by asking about problems which they may have overlooked such as drunken driving, traffic fines, police court records, and state traffic laws. The formula-tion of each question and its exact wording should be left to the pupils, who thus gain a vested interest in a problem they might otherwise con-sider dull. Such laissez-faire procedures presuppose that pupils have had preliminary training in analysis; breaking down a problem into specific contributory questions does not appear to be a natural child-hood skill, but it is one that students rapidly and eagerly master.

Gathering data, the third step in problem solving, takes the greatest amount of time. A class should be able to set up a survey in two or three class lessons; the collecting of data often takes three or four weeks. Pupils can easily be trained to use many or all of the follow-ing techniques in collecting data. These particular ones were used in a survey on bicycle traffic.

1. Bibliographical research
   a. available books on safety
   b. available current magazines, articles, and pamphlets
   c. old newspapers
   d. police court records
2. Note taking
3. Abstracting reports
4. Locating non-printed data
5. Interviewing
6. Conducting field surveys
   a. traffic counts
   b. checking mechanical safety
   c. investigating parking habits
   d. checking night-driving habits
7. Preparing, distributing, and checking questionnaires
8. Verifying sources of information

Most social studies teachers are acquainted with the instructional problems pertinent to each of these techniques. We have found that direct teaching produces much better results than merely trusting that our pupils are acquiring the necessary techniques indirectly. Thus, a day should be set aside for giving instruction in interviewing and conducting field surveys. Time spent on teaching techniques properly will be saved in the later stages of the work.

Organizing data is difficult for the average high school pupil to do well unless he has had direct teaching on how to organize materials.

He can collect masses of somewhat jumbled information in two or three weeks of intensive study. Perhaps he should be expected to arrange it and classify it as he goes along, but even when he does so he never gets a very clear idea of the ultimate purpose of his arrangement, and he often has to rearrange his material subsequently. The most we can expect is that in a problem like *How Can Traffic Accidents Be Controlled?* each student will keep his data filed under the relevant contributory problems. Organization of data from that point on means that the pupil will reclassify his findings and arrange them so that they will lead inevitably to three or four summary statements which he will be able to accept and defend. Teachers can save everyone's time by checking the relevancy of all data at this point.

The pupil and teacher should next discuss the most effective way of presenting the data in graphic form. The following procedures have been tested and found to be efficient: Have the data submitted in graphs and tables, checked for accuracy, supplemented by written explanation, and personalized by the pupil in some creative activity, such as writing, speaking, drawing, or acting. Although this creative activity is usually presented at a later stage in the survey, its form is often determined during the arrangement of the data. Here is ample opportunity for training and practice in oral and written English and in the mathematical skills.

In synthesizing data the information which has been gathered and arranged is crystallized into three or four generalizations. This part of the survey affords ample opportunity for the teacher to discuss the higher mental processes which permit human beings to make generalizations from specific cases. Here, too, is the time when social studies teachers can demonstrate to pupils the nature of proof. In fact, the most difficult technique in the scientific method of attacking problems lies in synthesizing data. Pupils enjoy this and the succeeding step in the process more than any other when the steps are properly developed.

Formulation of an hypothesis demands that the generalizations agreed upon in the preceding step be crystallized still further into one inclusive generalization of an hypothetical nature. The hypothesis resulting from the Traffic Survey was "Traffic signals should be placed at two new intersections."

Verification demands that the pupil submit his findings and hypothesis to the best available authority for inspection and criticism. Pupils in the Traffic Survey discussed their findings with the city committee on safety, who verified their report. In many instances the "best available authority" will be the teacher of the class or a local citizen who will evaluate the validity of the data and the steps leading to the generalization.

Forming a conclusive and defensible generalization frequently means merely making the minute changes in the hypothesis which were suggested by the authority consulted. The hypothesis may have to be radically changed or reconstructed before it can be accepted. The amount of change necessary is often inversely proportional to the amount of teacher domination present in the formulation of the hypothesis. It is probably best to have the students work out their own conclusions and revise them later if necessary.

Acting upon the generalization is the final step. Any survey implies that the study will be completed only when some change in community life has been made or when one aspect of present community life is discovered to be satisfactory. Pupils in the traffic survey completed their work when they encouraged the city council to remove traffic hazards. Not all surveys terminate so properly and so neatly, but no school would want to conduct one fruitless study after another. Sooner or later community analysis must lead to definite action.

The problem solving method provides an abundance of academic training for pupils who participate seriously. All the essential skills of learning can be called into play in any community survey. In fact, the work provides a real-life situation for the practice of skills previously learned. Functional as this training in the learning skills may be, the training in social skills is even more significant.

In conducting a community survey, pupils are constantly called upon to give evidence of healthy social development. It is not always easy for an adolescent to interview an adult gracefully, but students can learn to do so with practice. Pupils in our school are constantly complimented upon their excellent manners and their ease in meeting older people. We have some evidence that this can be attributed to the training they are given in interviewing.

Conducting a survey affords pupils an opportunity to observe human behavior. Before we send a group of pupils out into the community, we analyse all the possible situations in which they might find themselves. Pupils are selected to act the part of intolerant adults, busy adults, incredulous adults, cantankerous adults, magnanimous but skeptical adults, and completely cooperative adults. The types are analysed and pupils are taught how to meet each kind of person.

Leaving school for an afternoon encourages pupils to attend to their personal appearance, the charm of their voices, and the total impression their appearance creates. Pupils gain confidence through these experiences; and finally, in public presentations before school assemblies, city council meeting, safety council meetings, and public forums, they acquire a sense of their potential worth to the world. They stand up before the city and speak, not opinions, but facts as they have found them. The dignity of such a performance does fine things to the personality of almost every pupil who experiences it.

The most significant outcome of participation in community problems lies in the genesis of a healthier attitude toward government. Pupils who have studied a local problem at first hand, collected original data, formulated their own opinions about the problem, and presented their opinions to a governing agency have had an experience in citizenship that no other form of education can afford. If, in addition, the local government acts upon the pupils' recommendations, a precedent has been established which encourages these pupils to further participation. Perhaps when these school children become adults, they will retain their faith in government and their enthusiasm for participation. Community surveys are not educational panaceas; they will probably never replace history or civics; but they do offer any school an opportunity to make social education vital.

Detailed Analysis of the Bicycle Survey

Perhaps the most effective way of understanding these theories as they operate in teaching practice is to follow a typical survey from its inception to its conclusion.

A member of the city council visited the school last year and asked us to make an extensive study of the bicycle problem in Greeley. Several accidents and numerous complaints had made the city suspicious of prevailing practices. The social studies department agreed to conduct a survey of the problem in Greeley and in other cities of similar size. The city council offered to defray the expenses of the survey, but the department refused the offer on the grounds that the school is a public institution supported by taxation and at the service of the community generally. Much of the success of this survey sprang from the fact that the problem was real, it had social

significance, and pupils could do something about it when they concluded their survey.

Three eleventh grade pupils were selected on the basis of interest
as the general coordinators of the survey. In their first meeting
together they defined the problem as *What Regulations Should
Govern Bicycle Traffic in Greeley?* In two subsequent meetings they
determined the following subsidiary problems:

> What written material is already available for the city council?
> What laws prevail in other cities the size of Greeley?
> To what extent are Greeley bicycles mechanically safe?
> What are the danger spots for bicycle traffic?
> What laws are necessary for night traffic?
> Should bicycles be ridden in the street or on the sidewalks?

Collecting data pertaining to these problems was the next task
facing the students. The first question was answered by a comprehensive study of all available safety literature. This problem was
the first one started and the last one completed because of the fact that
new material kept arriving. The second problem was attacked by
means of a form letter requesting information which was mailed to
one hundred cities approximately the same size as Greeley. *The Census Abstracts* provided a list of cities throughout the United States.
Eighty-two percent of the cities written to responded with relevant
information.

In order to obtain data on the question concerning the mechanical
safety of Greeley bicycles, a check list was built covering the significant features of a bicycle. This list was submitted to three bicycle
dealers and considerably amended by them, much to the surprise and
information of the students. The revised list was then mimeographed
and two hundred copies run. Two hundred bicycles were checked
by the pupils, who selected four centers at which to work: a junior
high school parking rack, a senior high school parking rack, a combined junior-senior high school rack, and the rack in front of the
theatre which runs Saturday afternoon western thrillers for children.
Care was taken to avoid duplication. At the end of this part of the
survey, the pupils were able to identify ten or twelve bicycles which
were definitely a menace to their riders and other people. The group
was also able to derive significant generalizations from the data they
received.

Data on the fourth question, *What are the danger spots for bicycle
traffic?* was obtained by checking police court records of bicycle ac-

cidents, and by observing intersections and areas thus identified as dangerous. The coordinating committee delegated a group of younger pupils to conduct this portion of the survey.

The problem of what regulations are essential for safety in bicycling suggested four new sources of interesting data. Questionnaires were distributed to a hundred motorists and a hundred housewives, asking them to suggest the laws they considered necessary to control bicycle traffic. Interviews were conducted with junior high school and senior high school pupils, and with all the newspaper carriers and telegraph boys. As a final check, pupils from the lower levels wrote to thirty large cities for their suggestions and conducted fifty on-the-street interviews with citizens selected at random.

Data thus collected was next arranged in logical order under the problem heading to which it pertained. Many letters from cities were used in several places, because they frequently contained printed material, copies of their own regulations, and gratuitous suggestions. Statistical data derived from check lists, traffic counts, questionnaires, and interviews was recorded in bar graphs of contrasting colors. Tables showing conflicting local opinions were constructed. Regulations in general use throughout the United States were codified. Suggestions that did not fall into any of these categories were tabulated under the heading "miscellaneous."

Synthesis of the data received was perhaps the most difficult part of the whole study. Deductions were drawn from the information at hand and the entire procedure written up and checked at every point. This writing and checking consumed several weeks. In another type of survey the synthesis might have been accomplished in less time.

An hypothesis was then formulated. The pupils felt that in the light of their evidence (1) bicycles should be ridden only in the streets; (2) bicycles should be checked more frequently and the dangerously deficient ones removed from use; (3) careful police check should be made upon the practices of all after-dark bicycle riders. As in many social studies surveys, the verification of this hypothesis lay in the validity of the sources of information used and in the honesty of the tabulation. No one in Greeley could verify this hypothesis, because the students who made it had at their disposal much more information concerning bicycles than any readily available authority.

At the conclusion of the survey the pupils presented their findings in five distinct ways. (1) They reported to the safety council of the city and discussed the whole problem of bicycle traffic with that council and with the police department, making two specific suggestions that were subsequently adopted by the city. (2) They rented a moving picture about bicycles and showed it widely throughout the schools, indicating the dangerous practices that might result in fatal accidents. (3) They conducted a panel discussion before sixty members of a local luncheon club, who cross-questioned them for half an hour, and who supported their conclusions concerning bicycles. (4) They conducted panel discussions before elementary school children. (5) They constructed colorful graphs, wrote interesting comments, printed a neat design on typing paper, typed all their findings, and bound them together in a book which will serve as a guide and a standard for future community surveys. This work is now being used as the basic reference for junior high school students who are studying safe bicycle driving.

The itemized cost of the bicycle survey was:

Stencil and 200 copies of the check list ....$	.75
Stencil and 100 copies of form letter to cities	.50
Three stencils and fifty copies each of junior high questionnaires ..	1.10
Stencil and 200 copies of form letter to cities	.75
Stencil and 200 copies of questionnaire to citizens	.75
100 envelopes	.20
Postage for 100 letters	3.00
Rental fee for a commercial film	2.00
Damage to the film	2.00
Cost of binding a book made by the students	.75
	$11.80

This is the most expensive survey we have made, but if we wished we could have had all expenses paid by the community. We spent a sum of money that might have purchased five textbooks. For that money our pupils had a thrilling experience, our school served the community, and we now have a typewritten book illustrating the procedures to be followed in conducting a community survey.

Community Surveys in the Typical School

Many social studies departments that might like to duplicate such a program of community participation in their schools are deterred by one or all of three problems. The first of these disquieting questions is easy to answer. *Does every community present an opportunity for such education?* The necessary data for such surveys is certainly available in every American community. Every fire department, every traffic court, every police department, every social or economic activity, is a living repository for social studies data. There may be some communities that will not want students to study such data, or that will react coldly to public presentations of what the pupils find. Unsympathetic communities surely do exist, but they appear to be far less numerous than teachers often suppose.

The second question we can answer more definitely. *Is not the cost of such education prohibitive?* By careful bookkeeping we have tried to estimate the cost of such projects in our school. Our table shows that it is possible to keep the costs of a long survey down to less than a dollar in actual money spent. Of course, such a survey would probably have been better had more money been available. More trips would have made the work more interesting. Ten dollars in cash would be ample, as we have demonstrated, for any extensive survey of a community problem.

One reason why our expenses are kept so low is the considerable library of reference materials built up by our school over a number of years. We do not have to spend part of our survey expense fund each time on basic standard references. Eight dollars will buy, however, the six most used reference books. Any school would find the following inexpensive yearbooks satisfactory as a nucleus around which to build a constantly growing reference library.

Agricultural Statistics	$ .50
Census Abstracts	1.50
Commerce Yearbook	2.00
Statistical Abstracts	1.50
World Almanac	.50
State Yearbook (estimated)	2.00

The first four may be purchased from the Superintendent of Documents, Washington, D.C., the *World Almanac* from any bookseller, and the state yearbook from any state bureau of publications.

A further method by which to secure inexpensive source material from which pupils can acquire data is by the constant use of pamphlet materials. The social studies department of the Secondary School of Colorado State College of Education experimented this year with the use of two dollars worth of postal cards. By sending them judiciously to business houses, propaganda agencies, advertising concerns, national committees, and whatever other sources of free material appeared promising, we secured for our two dollars a filing cabinet full of materials, about sixty-five percent of which will be useful in our teaching. Had we allowed five dollars for the purchase of inexpensive supplementary pamphlets as well, we could have built a respectable library of pamphlet materials for seven dollars. The National Council for the Social Studies lists many sources of relevant pamphlet material in its Bulletin No. 8, *Pamphlets on Public Affairs for Use in Social Studies Classes,* by Kronenberg, Tryon, and Nutter. The United States Office of Education has a bibliography costing ten cents which gives sources of free pamphlets. No school need fear that the cost of community surveys will be prohibitive. Instead, the costs are often less than the price a school pays for one copy of a good textbook.

The last and most serious doubt which might deter other schools from following this program is: *Do the students learn anything?* When we started our community surveys citizens used to say that "they didn't see what good a bunch of kids can do running around the streets." Other educators made the same comment. Now, when our program functions so well that the community itself requests us to work for it, such criticisms are infrequent. At least the patrons of the school are willing to support us in our surveys.

Popular approval, however, is no substitute for scientific proof. So far we have only subjective observations and student responses to rely upon. We cannot measure the social responsibility of a pupil who has worked on surveys and compare the result with the social responsibility demonstrated by a student who never worked on one. We offer the following subjective evidence: (1) We have no difficulty in getting students to work on second and third surveys after they have once participated in the various experiences connected with solving their first interesting community problem. (2) Our pupils are constantly being complimented by adults outside the school for their courtesy, social intelligence, and interest in community life. (3) Pupils who participate in surveys appear to improve in initiative and in self-confidence in social situations. (4) Pupils have always been able to prepare neat written reports and to deliver charming oral reports. (5) We have some objective evidence to prove that pupils who use and comprehend the steps in problem-solving learn to think more rationally than pupils who have not been introduced to scientific thinking. This end might, however, be accomplished by using the problem solving method unattached to a community survey.

PARTICIPATION IN COMMUNITY SURVEYS   163

If subjective evidence can be admitted in evaluating an educational program, we have proved to our own satisfaction that the community survey is a worthy enterprise in so far as the pupil is concerned. If objective evidence alone is valid, we can cite data upon the community's reception of our work which will prove that surveys are good for the school. Newspapers, public forums, hardheaded politicians, other schools, luncheon clubs, and social service societies have all applauded our students. If problem surveys achieve nothing else, they certainly improve school and community relationships.

JAMES A.
MICHENER
ON THE SOCIAL STUDIES

The Problem of the Social Studies

in
The Future of the Social Studies
Curriculum Series: Number One, 1939
James A. Michener, Editor
National Council for the Social Studies
Pages 1-5

" There is nothing inherently faulty in varied courses of study; on the contrary, variety is to be desired in democratic education. The Commission on the Social Studies, in refusing to deliver a ready-made curriculum became an agent in the revitalization of the social studies. ...Fortunately, one does not have to pass a value judgment on the curriculum movement in recent years, but on the whole it has probably done considerably more good than harm. One nevertheless should question certain aspects of the results.

Is it efficient to have each social-studies division construct its own curriculum?

Does individual curriculum construction produce satisfactory courses of study?

How can local curriculum committees avoid the more serious mistakes inherent in individual curriculum construction? "

The Problem of the Social Studies

JAMES A. MICHENER

THE purpose of this book would be misunderstood if its provisional nature were not kept constantly in mind. The National Council for the Social Studies would regret having this publication interpreted as a formal statement of what the social-studies curriculum should be. Instead, this is a collection of carefully prepared individual proposals concerning the curriculum. Each author has been invited to state briefly his conception of what the social-studies course of study should be in the immediate future.

These proposals, therefore, represent the reasoned judgment of men and women whose professional life has for the most part been spent in considering the problems of the social studies. As individual articles, each merits the closest study, for each has behind it a fortifying wealth of scholarship, experience, and conviction; but the total volume remains merely an attempt to assemble in one place samples of the best modern thinking on the social-studies curriculum.

The ideal course of study cannot be determined by taking each of these fifteen proposals, finding out what each writer says should be taught in Grade III, determining the proposal which was made most often, and announcing that here is the answer for Grade III. Each of these curricula is an organic whole and has been planned to be administered as such. Several of the curricula are already in use substantially as here outlined; others represent composite practice, but each is essentially a workable plan of procedure.

WHY THIS BOOK WAS WRITTEN

The principal problems connected with the social studies have frequently been divided into six general areas. (1) Decide upon the objectives for which the social studies will be taught. (2) Construct courses which will attain these objectives. (3) Select and arrange the necessary materials for use in these courses. (4) Determine what methods shall be used. (5) Prepare teachers to administer the courses thus established. (6) Evaluate the entire procedure.

Each of these six important fields is being studied carefully today, but certain areas have progressed much further toward a satisfactory solution than have others. For example, objectives have been the subject of much study. At present it seems likely that the major objectives stated in *Purposes of Education in American Democracy* will be accepted by most curriculum-makers.[1] These objectives are not significantly different from those inferred in the *Conclusions and Recommendations* of the last national committee which considered the social studies.[2] Wirth has gathered together much of the available research on social-studies objectives and has tabulated his findings in usable form.[3] It is probably correct to say that there is ample guidance for anyone wishing to reconsider or restudy the problem of objectives for the social studies.

Materials for teaching are also being improved constantly. Individual textbooks are reaching an unusually high standard of utility. Series of texts representing integrated or correlated materials for several consecutive years are also available. Several publishers are experimenting with pamphlets containing individual units, so that the teacher may soon be able to select from a wide variety the particular sequence of units he wishes to teach in

[1] National Education Association. Educational Policies Commission, *Purposes of Education in American Democracy.* Washington, D.C.: National Education Association, 1938.

[2] *Conclusions and Recommendations.* Part XVI: Report of the Commission on the Social Studies, American Historical Association. New York: Charles Scribner's Sons, 1934.

[3] Fremont P. Wirth, "Objectives for the Social Studies," Chapter II of National Council for the Social Studies, *Eighth Yearbook: The Contribution of Research to the Teaching of the Social Studies.* Cambridge, Mass.: The Secretary, 1937.

any one year. Particularly noteworthy are the new source books that are appearing. Some are centered around special fields of interest, such as the westward movement or the documents of history, whereas others endeavor to provide the teacher with maximum illustrative social material for an entire year's work. Visual and auditory aids such as maps, moving pictures, and radio programs are also being constantly improved.

The field of methods for the social studies has become fairly well organized. Most schools of education are advocating that teachers break their work down into manageable segments and that they teach these segments according to well defined procedures. Activity is assuming its proper place in method, and the principles of democratic classroom practice have been fairly well agreed upon, even though actual performance still lags behind our knowledge of what to do.

The preparation of competent teachers is being studied widely, and those practices which promise to produce better teachers are rapidly spreading. The American Council on Education's Commission on Teacher Education is at present concerned with this problem, and in the field of the social studies the most recent yearbook of the National Council deals directly with teacher education.[4] Likewise in evaluation there is a fairly clear understanding of desirable procedures. Anderson, Lindquist, Wrightstone, and Tyler have done much to provide teachers with clearly stated principles governing evaluation. These men and others have also prepared evaluation instruments that can be used in most social-studies classrooms.

In fact, there is agreement as to what the social studies should accomplish. Usable materials are at hand; methods are being improved; teachers are being prepared to use the newer methods; and evaluation instruments have been perfected to test whether or not the whole process is efficient. If practice in these fields lags behind accepted theory, it is not because acceptable theory is not available; but for the questions of *what to teach* and *when to teach it* there are no clear answers.

THE SOCIAL-STUDIES CURRICULUM TODAY

No longer can a "Committee of Seven" promulgate a history curriculum which the majority of schools will accept.[5] Realizing this, the most recent national committee, the Commission on the Social Studies of the American Historical Association, refrained from suggesting a detailed curriculum. Their hesitancy was properly interpreted by the schools to mean that a period of wide experimentation was about to ensue. True, experimentation had already started in many schools, but the ubiquitous "Social-Studies Curriculum Committee" of recent years largely grew out of the Commission's *Conclusions and Recommendations*. Krey's short volume, *A Regional Program for the Social Studies*,[6] to some extent gave impetus to local curriculum groups, for in his essay Krey made a point which will probably gain continued prominence in the social studies, namely: American society tends to be understood best when broken down into the regional areas that comprise it. A logical development of such a thesis is that each region should construct its own curriculum.

The College Entrance Examination Board published its report on examinations in such a way as to imply a social-studies curriculum that could be largely satisfactory if administered by very well prepared teachers,[7] and the forthcoming social-studies publications of the Progressive Education Association[8] will also imply a curriculum without presenting one.

[4] National Council for the Social Studies, *Tenth Yearbook: In-Service Growth of Social-Studies Teachers.* Cambridge, Mass.: The Secretary, 1939.

[5] It is interesting to note that even this most influential of committee reports was not able to command unanimous support. See Rolla M. Tryon, *The Social Sciences as School Subjects.* Part XI: The Report of the Commission on the Social Studies, American Historical Association. New York: Charles Scribner's Sons, 1935.

[6] A. C. Krey, *A Regional Program for the Social Studies.* New York: The Macmillan Company, 1938.

[7] "Final Report and Recommendations of the Commission on History to the College Entrance Examination Board," *The Social Studies,* 27:546-566 (December, 1936). Also published in pamphlet form. College Entrance Examination Board, 431 West 117th Street, New York City.

[8] *The Social Studies in General Education,* mimeographed revision of June, 1939. New York: The Progressive Education Association.

JAMES A. MICHENER 3

The state-wide curriculum initiated in Virginia has encouraged radical revision of social-studies curricula elsewhere, for the Virginia curriculum centers upon a fascinating central core of social-studies material.[9] Publication of vigorously revised social-studies courses of study by departments of education in Texas, Michigan, and elsewhere will add further impetus to widespread revision.

What will the conclusion of this experimentation be? According to the latest figures, Teachers College, Columbia University, has on file more than 50,000 separate courses of study. Some alarm has been felt because one western state reported thirty-seven different social-studies courses being taught in the last three years of high school. Most educators would prefer thirty-seven different courses to one rigid sequence from which there was no deviation; but the continued multiplicity of social-studies courses of study raises several questions. One must admit there is needless duplication. Are there other questionable factors?

THE VALIDITY OF THE CURRICULUM

There is nothing inherently faulty in varied courses of study; on the contrary, variety is to be desired in democratic education. The Commission on the Social Studies, in refusing to deliver a ready-made curriculum became an agent in the revitalization of the social studies. One has only to read Harper's dismal report of what has been happening to history to appreciate the fact that almost any infusion of red corpuscles into the curriculum was desirable.[10] There is ample evidence of the benefits that accrue to teachers who have the good fortune to work on curriculum committees and who are forced to reconsider the principles upon which they have been teaching. Fortunately, one does not have to pass a value judgment on the curriculum movement in recent years, but on the whole it has probably done considerably more good than harm. One nevertheless should question certain aspects of the result.

Is it efficient to have each social-studies division construct its own curriculum? There is a temptation to say "no," but anyone who has watched a school spring to life under the impetus of curriculum revision must honestly say that even were a curriculum all printed and ready to be implemented, it would be preferable for the teachers themselves to experience the pleasure and the responsibility of building their own. This is merely another example of the fact that democratic procedures are not always the most efficient, in so far as external measures are concerned.

Does individual curriculum construction produce satisfactory courses of study? Unfortunately, when the thrill of constructing a curriculum has worn off, schools often find themselves saddled with monstrosities. Several recent courses of study produced by isolated schools have represented nothing but surrender once more to what Dodd calls "history's imperialistic claim." It seemed evident that the social-studies teachers who constructed those courses of study had either never heard of the *Conclusions and Recommendations*, or having heard of them, had relegated them to oblivion. On the other hand, three recent courses of study for secondary schools contained no history whatever, the social studies being represented by a mass of poorly organized and largely unteachable conglomerates. Haphazard courses of studies for the social studies are usually repetitious, frequently lacking in integration, and oftentimes purely capricious in choice of subject matter. Such courses constantly ignore the newer materials on childhood growth and development, and in the latter years particularly fail to take into consideration the valuable material that is being collected on student needs and interests.

How can local curriculum committees avoid the more serious mistakes inherent in individual curriculum construction? A social-studies course of study should be constructed

[9] Virginia State Board of Education, *Tentative Course of Study for Virginia Elementary Schools*. Richmond, Virginia; The Board, 1934.

[10] Charles A. Harper, "Why Do Children Dislike History?" *Social Education*, 1:492-494 (October, 1937).

only after considerable research and only when care is taken that it conforms to reasonable criteria. These criteria are not iron-clad restrictions threatening progress; instead, conformity to them would go far toward insuring liberal courses of study. To ignore them is to run the risk of producing merely one more capricious guess. Wesley has summarized the basic principles governing curriculum construction.[11] A statement of the general principles is contained in the *Fourteenth Yearbook* of the Department of Superintendence, and is quoted by Anderson elsewhere in this publication.[12] Both the *Fourth* and *Sixth Yearbooks* of the National Council for the Social Studies contain rational analyses of the social-studies curriculum.[13] Schutte deals with the problem in a broad philosophical manner,[14] and the Progressive Education Association establishes further standards for curriculum construction.[15] In addition to these works dealing exclusively with the social studies, there are numerous other works of a general nature, a hasty study of which would prevent many of the premature courses of study appearing today.

Does this publication help to clarify the problem? Of itself, it does not, but it was not meant to be an authoritative statement concerning what the social-studies curriculum should be. It is merely the first step in what may become a sustained effort to bring some order into a confused field. Here one has a picture of what several scholars envision the future of the social studies to be. It is hoped that these statements will form the basis of much serious discussion, and that from such discussion plans can be made for a commission which will consider the future of the social studies in the curriculum of American schools.

SOME INSISTENT PROBLEMS THAT MUST BE ANSWERED

In constructing a social-studies course of study, or even when considering the question of the social studies abstractly, several annoying problems arise that must be answered before one can honestly proceed to make any decisions. Anyone considering the social studies today must be aware of the following questions for which there are at present no clear-cut answers.

A course or a collection of classes. Up to the present few schools have really had a social-studies course; instead they have had a collection of individual classes which were supposed to integrate roughly on the basis of the report of the Committee of Seven as modified by the Committee on Social Studies of 1916 and the Committee on History and Education for Citizenship. A social-studies course implies a twelve-grade sequence of carefully integrated experiences leading to a clearly understood objective.

A multiple course of study. Social-studies teachers will soon have to make a very difficult decision. In fact, many are already faced with the dilemma of fitting old courses to a new situation. Secondary-school population will soon be radically changed if unemployment and the extension of compulsory school attendance continue. This means that considerable numbers of students for whom history, economics, and sociology as taught at present are unsuitable will demand attention. At the same time there is considerable justified apprehension concerning the fate of the very able student who can profit from advanced courses in the social sciences. It appears to many that such students are being cheated when schools make no provision for the traditional and potentially invigorating courses in history and the other social sciences. It may well be that the social studies will be forced to adopt a dual or even a multiple course of study.

The core curriculum. In many schools the core program is absorbing much of the social studies. This is not necessarily regrettable, but it would be a waste of long accumulated experience if the

[11] Edgar B. Wesley, *Teaching the Social Studies*. Boston: D. C. Heath, 1937, pp. 145-285.

[12] National Education Association, Department of Superintendence, *Fourteenth Yearbook: The Social-Studies Curriculum*. Washington, D.C.: National Education Association, 1936. Pp. 138-140. Quoted in Howard R. Anderson, "An Experimental Program in Social Studies for Grades I-XII," *infra* p. 18.

[13] National Council for the Social Studies, *Fourth Yearbook: The Social-Studies Curriculum*. Cambridge, Mass.: The Secretary, 1934.

National Council for the Social Studies, *Sixth Yearbook: Elements of the Social-Studies Program*. Cambridge, Mass.: The Secretary, 1936.

[14] T. H. Schutte, *Teaching the Social Studies on the Secondary School Level*. New York: Prentice-Hall, Inc., 1938. Pp. 247-317.

[15] *The Social Studies in General Education, op. cit.*

social studies were not to find a sensible place in this program. It may possibly be that in typical schools of the future there will be no social-studies department, but if such a decision is made, it should be made consciously, and not by default.

Social development. This is a most pressing problem for the social-studies teacher. On the one hand there is the school which delegates to social-studies courses all responsibility for the social development of students; whereas another school restricts its teachers to preparing children for rigorous external examinations on the facts of history, civics, and geography. Similarly, there are social-studies teachers who arrogate to themselves the whole job of caring for the social development of their students; whereas others seem offended if they are held in any way responsible for what children do outside the classroom. Quite probably the social studies will suffer if its curriculum or its teachers adopt either of these extreme alternatives, but the middle course through this confusion of responsibility is by no means clearly defined.

Civic education for an age of change. Social-studies curriculum-makers must soon decide just how sincerely they believe that their field can contribute to the education of young men and women who in all probability will face and live through a life of rather continuous change. Specifically, how important is training in democracy? Shall children be taught the necessity for certain economic readjustments? Shall the social studies undertake the difficult task of encouraging students to consider objectively the alternatives to present political patterns? Shall children be taught to adjust to the alternately minor and major sociological disruptions at present under way? Shall the social studies assume direct responsibility for the inculcation of the habits of good citizenship?

Indoctrination. However one answers the preceding questions, the problems of indoctrination, persuasion, and emotionalization are bound to enter into the discussions. Anyone constructing a social-studies curriculum today must consider very carefully the probable future of emotionalized learning.

Some specific questions concerning content. And finally there are many somewhat less inclusive problems concerning whether one will or will not include the study of new problems that seem to relate to the social studies. The following are illustrative: (1) If present tendencies toward centralization of authority and at the same time enhancement of local responsibility continue, the community will play an increasingly important rôle in national life. Shall community study center in and be planned for by the social studies? (2) Shall the new viewpoints in history, economics, geography, sociology, and the other social sciences be incorporated into the course of study? (3) Shall the co-operative movement be studied? (4) Shall the study of United States foreign policy be extended so as to include ample treatment of South America and Asia? (5) Shall the difficult problems of growth, emotional maturation, group behavior, and marriage find a place in the social studies? (6) Shall the social studies attempt to deal with the most urgent problem facing many young people, the place of youth in American life? (7) Shall the social-studies course of study make specific provision for the teaching of necessary skills?

The problem of the social studies is to find the most satisfactory answers to the questions that have been raised in this introduction. The following pages contain many excellent suggestions, and it is reassuring to note that among these writers there is considerable agreement concerning many phases of the curriculum. The long period of experimentation has produced a basic body of understandings upon which most social-studies people are beginning to agree. The specific implementation of these understandings still varies from writer to writer and from school to school. Few educators would wish to destroy these variants by imposing a rigid national curriculum; but it is also true that we are approaching the time when the social-studies curriculum can profitably incorporate those practices which have been found to be productive.

The next step should properly be a careful scrutiny of the proposals contained in this volume and elsewhere in an effort to determine what procedures hold the greatest promise for social studies in American schools. What is done with the information thus obtained will to a large degree determine the future of the social studies.

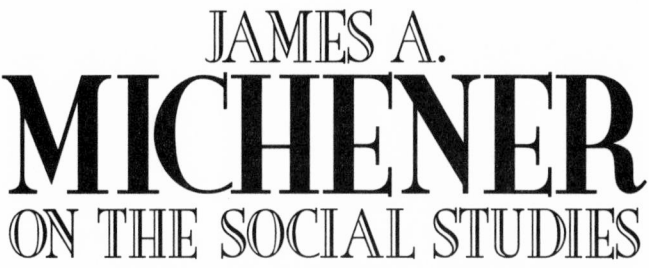

JAMES A. MICHENER
ON THE SOCIAL STUDIES

The Beginning Teacher
Chapter I

in

In-Service Growth of Social Studies Teachers
Tenth Yearbook 1939
Burr W. Phillips, Editor
National Council for the Social Studies
Pages 1-37

" This chapter is addressed primarily to those young men and women who are beginning their professional careers and who are determined to be more than just average teachers of the social studies. The standards herein proposed are unusually high. They are standards, however, which appear to be met by the leaders in the field. The author has no apologies for exhorting beginning teachers to strive to meet a high level of teaching and general professional conduct. For two excellent reasons the beginning teacher should set his goal high: (1) today more than ever before the schools of our nation need excellent teachers of the social studies; (2) there seems to be evidence that success, both professionally and financially, goes to such teachers. "

CHAPTER I

THE BEGINNING TEACHER

JAMES A. MICHENER

This chapter is addressed primarily to those young men and women who are beginning their professional careers and who are determined to be more than just average teachers of the social studies. The standards herein proposed are unusually high. They are standards, however, which appear to be met by the leaders in the field. The author has no apologies for exhorting beginning teachers to strive to meet a high level of teaching and general professional conduct. For two excellent reasons the beginning teacher should set his goal high: (1) today more than ever before the schools of our nation need excellent teachers of the social studies; (2) there seems to be evidence that success, both professionally and financially, goes to such teachers.

Insofar as possible, the contentions of this chapter will be substantiated by reference to research findings. Whenever personal opinion intrudes, that opinion will be identified. Beginning teachers should early acquire the habit of referring to research for information concerning their professional problems.

IS THERE AN IDEAL SOCIAL STUDIES TEACHER?

It is difficult to describe the ideal teacher. The art of great teaching is a chimerical thing which sometimes eludes analysis. Let an investigator identify a characteristic which he believes basic to good teaching, and immediately a score of excellent instructors can be found who ignore his precept. Teaching is individual; creative teaching establishes its own rules. Yet there are standards which most excellent teachers meet. We know a great deal about the differences between good teachers and poor teachers.

Several studies have been made of this problem. From them we can construct a description of the ideal social studies teacher. Beginning teachers need no longer drift idly through their profession for want of a concise statement of an ideal toward which they should be progressing. The author would be the first to encourage a beginning teacher to deviate from a rigid norm, but there is, nevertheless, a pleasing agreement as to what constitutes the ideal.

The starting point should probably be E. P. Smith's excellent short statement. Smith visited 101 social studies teachers whom consensus of opinion and objective analysis identified as superior. He reported to the American Historical Association's Commission on the Social Studies concerning the common attributes of these teachers. His findings coincide with what other investigators have found. He describes the outstanding teacher of the social studies by listing the following attributes:

1. Reverence for Truth
2. Intelligent Optimism
3. Social Altruism
4. Sympathy
5. Impartiality
6. Interpretive Mind
7. Progressiveness
8. Curiosity
9. Culture
10. Imagination
11. Dramatic Instinct
12. Selective Mind
13. Balance
14. Vigorous Personality
15. Tactfulness
16. Ability to Inspire Confidence
17. Loyalty to Ideals[1]

Nearly every great teacher of the social studies possesses these attributes at least to a limited degree. One might well conclude that a beginning teacher who gave evidence of revering the truth, of having an intelligent optimism, and so on through the list, would have good prospects of becoming a master teacher in his field.

Barr surveyed the work of 47 social studies teachers generally agreed to be poor and compared it with the practice of 47 teachers who were generally rated superior. This study was conducted pragmatically, with only overt behavior catalogued, but the results coincide in part with Smith's. The good teacher:

1. Is interested in what his pupils say and do.
2. Uses illustrative material frequently to elucidate points in discussion.
3. Knows his subject matter.
4. Gives precise, meaningful assignments.
5. Encourages pupils to keep good notebooks.
6. Administers a wide outside-reading program.
7. Uses examinations intelligently.

[1] Edward Payson Smith, "A Study of Personal Qualities Essential in a Superior Teacher of the Social Studies," in W. C. Bagley and Thomas Alexander, *The Teacher of the Social Studies*, Part XIV: Report of the Commission on the Social Studies, p. 251. New York: Charles Scribner's Sons, 1937.

THE BEGINNING TEACHER 3

8. Uses a conversational manner.
9. Has at his command a wealth of commentary statements.
10. Encourages pupils to use their own experiences in discussion.
11. Has a good technique in asking questions.
12. Is able to stimulate interest in whatever he is teaching.
13. Uses the socialized recitation.
14. Uses supervised study instead of all outside assignments.
15. Demonstrates a willingness to experiment.[2]

In Barr's study the emphasis is upon method and procedure, rather than upon personality and mental traits. Yet it is probable that the type of teacher described by Smith would almost automatically do the things Barr's good teachers did. One should check Barr's list against Smith's to see how often Barr gives the specific teaching technique that implements Smith's summarizing characteristic. For example, Smith says that the able teacher has an interpretive mind. Barr says that the good teacher of the social studies uses illustrative material and has a wealth of commentary statements.

The *Conclusions and Recommendations* of the American Historical Association's Commission on the Social Studies describes briefly the ideal social studies teacher as an individual combining "high scholarship, courage, and vision, and inspired by a love of knowledge and mankind."[3]

A very able description of a teacher who approached the ideal implied in these various reports was given several years ago in an informal letter. The description is still apt.

And always, no matter whether we were studying past history or present, she wanted to know what we thought and why we thought it. I can remember how happy she used to look when we would get into an excited discussion of some subject on which we disagreed, and how she always disliked to put an end to it. I suppose it was because she knew that we were on these occasions really interested. . . . But I think that the one thing that made all these other things mean so much to us was that we knew Miss B really cared about us; that no matter how much she cared about history, it was her pupils who made the most difference to her. If any of us failed to do his best work, she really felt badly about it, not for the work's sake or her own, but for ours. She always made us feel that she could not be satisfied until every one of us was doing the very best he

[2] A. S. Barr, *Characteristic Differences in the Teaching Performance of Good and Poor Teachers of the Social Studies*. Bloomington, Illinois: Public School Publishing Company, 1929. p. 68.

[3] American Historical Association, Commission on the Social Studies, *Conclusions and Recommendations*. New York: Charles Scribner's Sons, 1934. p. 118.

could do. She never was too busy, or too interested in her own affairs, to give us the help we needed. She was always as courteous to us as to the superintendent or any one else, for courtesy wasn't put on for the occasion; it was a part of her, and we were of more importance to her than any one else around. Some way, too, she made us know that the thing she cared most about was character, and she made it easier to do right because she believed in us and trusted us.[4]

Wilson has recently given an excellent description of a good teacher at work in his classroom.

. . . One teacher was conducting a class of thirty-seven pupils in American history. The subject for the day was foreign relations of this country about 1900. The textbook material and current international relations were closely related. The teacher was very well informed, and his very competence in that respect seemed to lift the level of the discussion. For discussion it was, with the teacher almost a storm center of pupil activity. And the important element in the discussion was the way in which the teacher calmly, judiciously, and consistently refused to be "swept off his feet" by emotional blasts or by vague generalizations. Every erroneous or extravagant statement was challenged, if not by the pupils, then by the teacher. The entire discussion dealt with factual materials, but the facts were related to one another in terms of concepts, and the process was one in which straight thinking was taught and exemplified. In the hands of that teacher, routine rules for methodology were farcical; his procedure was intimate in the process of group thinking. But wherever teachers approaching his caliber as a thought-provoker were observed, they seemed to employ in large measure a procedure based upon fairly free and vivid verbal "give and take."[5]

Like previous analyses, Wilson's description of the excellent teacher is so simple that one wonders why all social studies teachers are not equally efficient. To the beginning teacher the simplicity that marks great teaching should be an encouragement. At present we can identify four characteristics that seem to be necessary for good social studies teaching.

1. Devotion to the truth, plus the will to have one's students discover and accept the truth.
2. Permanent, sincere concern with the various social processes in operation about one.
3. Social optimism, social altruism, and social participation.
4. The courage, the vision, and the determination to work for the perfection of the democratic principle.

[4] Monona L. Cheney, "An Ideal History Teacher." *The Historical Outlook*, December, 1924.

[5] Howard E. Wilson, *Education for Citizenship*. New York: McGraw-Hill Book Company, 1938. p. 169.

THE BEGINNING TEACHER 5

Other factors conditioning success will be identified in the next section. If the beginning teacher has none of the above qualities, he should read no further, for without some of these unifying ideals he will probably never be even a mediocre teacher of the social studies.

WILL I BE A SUCCESSFUL TEACHER?

It is possible that a beginning teacher might possess many of the characteristics of the ideal social studies teacher and still fail because of some other deficiency. Young teachers should appraise the likelihood of their success. Too often young men and women merely drift into teaching without any aptitude or vocation for the task. In time they become spiritless day laborers in the classroom. Totally unfitted for their task, they make learning dull and citizenship meaningless.

Unfortunately, there is no sure way by which one can determine his fitness for teaching. Ten extensive studies of predicting teaching success were carried on between 1906 and 1938. They produced no attribute which invariably predicted success. It is probably safe to say that no single quality determines success in teaching. This means that teaching, like most arts, is an occupation that can profitably absorb a wide variety of individuals.

Although there may be no single criterion predictive of success, there are several well established factors which generally accompany good teaching. At present it seems safe to say that successful teachers usually have some of the following characteristics:

1. They are well liked by their students.
2. They have a professional interest in teaching.
3. They possess an interesting, well adjusted personality.
4. They have the ability to cooperate in school life.
5. They usually made high marks in methods courses.
6. They had satisfactory marks in general college work.
7. They have above average native intelligence.[6]

Different studies emphasize different factors as predominately important, but most good teachers combine most of the seven characteristics. It seems obvious that a beginning teacher who possessed none of these qualities should hesitate about remaining with the profession.

[6] Frederick L. Whitney, *The Elements of Research*. New York: Prentice-Hall, Inc., 1937. p. 400. Adapted from "Rank Order of Thirty-eight Factors Related to Teaching Success." Modified by two subsequent studies.

There are other facts which the beginning teacher can consider when he makes his estimate of his own future. Hart asked 3,725 students to describe their best liked teacher. The ten most frequent responses were:

1. Is helpful with school work, explains lessons and assignments clearly and thoroughly, uses examples in teaching.
2. Cheerful, happy, good-natured, jolly, has a sense of humor, and can take a joke.
3. Human, friendly, companionable, "one of us."
4. Interested in and understands pupils.
5. Makes work interesting, creates a desire to work, makes class work a pleasure.
6. Strict, has control of the class, commands respect.
7. Impartial, shows no favoritism, has no "pets."
8. Not cross, crabby, grouchy, nagging, or sarcastic.
9. "We learned the subject."
10. A pleasing personality.[7]

Bond asked 1,400 teachers who were rated from bad to excellent to write descriptions of themselves. The significant difference between the good and the bad was that the good teachers prided themselves on their initiative, whereas the poor teachers felt that their colleges had not given them enough ready-made materials which they could teach to their children.[8]

The author of this chapter has reviewed the available studies of this problem and concludes that unusual success in teaching is usually compounded of five elements:

1. A positive philosophy of education.
2. Sufficient control of subject matter.
3. Varied methods of teaching.
4. Knowledge of children.
5. Good teaching personality.

This chapter will analyze briefly the last four of these components as they apply to social studies teachers; it will conclude by considering several specific problems germane to all teaching.

How Much Subject Matter Should I Know?

A knowledge of the social sciences is essential before a teacher can look for outstanding success in teaching the social studies to

---

[7] Frank W. Hart, *Teachers and Teaching*, New York: The Macmillan Company, 1934. p. 131.

[8] Jesse A. Bond, "Superior and Inferior Teachers: Their Similarities and Differences." *Phi Delta Kappan*, January, 1938.

THE BEGINNING TEACHER 7

elementary and secondary school students. Many of the abilities which have been agreed upon as components of good teaching imply the mastery of subject matter. Such enviable traits as timely illustration, clear explanation, biographical stories, illustration of geographical factors, and reference to historical similarities demand an ample background of subject matter. The teacher who has studied widely in the social sciences has a much better chance of becoming a challenging teacher than one who knows little or nothing of them. Of course, other factors are equally important if a beginning teacher is to succeed. He must know children, he must have excellent methods, and he must have a unifying philosophy; but even these desirable traits are of little consequence unless possessed by an individual who also knows what he is teaching.

The amount of subject matter needed for success in teaching has not been agreed upon. In fact, it is fashionable in some places to decry scholastic marks in their relationship to teaching. Beginning teachers are often told that "honor students never make good teachers" and that "the good, old, dependable C student is always the best teacher." A possible explanation of the prevalence of this point of view was given by Engelhardt in 1930.

Evidence now available appears to demonstrate fully that there is little if any correlation between teaching success and intelligence. This is not true in regard to success in fields of education taken as a whole, for as a rule the very able seek or are chosen to those positions which pay the highest salaries and which carry the greatest prestige. This practice will continue under present conditions in spite of the preference of many persons to classroom teaching. The organization of educational institutions, particularly the public schools as now operative, will continue to take superior teachers and endeavor to transform them into administrators, supervisors, and research specialists.[9]

The attack on subject matter is based upon the fact that every year a few brilliant students leave college knowing a great deal of history, or economics, or political science. Knowing little or nothing of children, methods, and the purposes of the school, these brilliant students often do a miserable job of teaching. Their failure seems worse because their prospects seemed so bright. They provide evidence for the belief that the really good teachers are themselves mediocre students.

[9] Fred Engelhardt, "Differentiation in Classroom Teaching." *Educational Administration and Supervision*, May, 1930.

This belief is merely a part of the American educational mythology. It is a generalization founded upon a few specific cases. The contention does not stand up under scrutiny. Knudsen and McAfee surveyed the studies dealing with intelligence and teaching success.

It has been said that people with moderate intelligence can teach better than those with superior intelligence. The latter often teach above the heads of their pupils. However, they can use their superior intelligence to study the methods of meeting the understanding of their pupils. Statistical correlations between evidences of intellectual ability and evidences of teaching success have not usually been very high, because the available evidences of both types of ability have not been very reliable. As a rule, the more objective and reliable the data, the higher the correlation between success as a student and success as a teacher. The prospective teacher's chances of rating high in teaching are better if his intelligence rating is high. The pupil's chance to learn has even been found to be better with a more intelligent teacher.[10]

A word of warning is necessary. This evidence does not say that mere possession of information is synonymous with good teaching. The evidence does not contend that the college student with high grades always becomes a good teacher. What it does say is what many thoughtful educators have known for a long time: intelligence and knowledge are not handicaps in teaching; in fact, they may be of great assistance if used correctly. The maladjusted teacher is always a poor teacher, whether his marks in college were A's or F's. The teacher with no techniques is usually dull and unsatisfactory, regardless of the information he may have at his command. The outstandingly successful social studies teacher has probably always been a unique blend of information, technique, philosophy, and sympathy.

Since we can prove that thorough knowledge of one's chosen field will not handicap a teacher, we can next logically ask how much a social studies teacher needs to know. The best answer seems to be that one can never know enough to teach this exhaustive field as well as he would like. The beginning teacher will generally have discrepancies in his preparation. From an analysis of the social studies as they are taught today, it would be ideal if every teacher were at least competent in the following social sciences:

[10] C. W. Knudsen and L. O. McAfee, *An Introduction to Teaching.* New York: Doubleday, Doran and Company, 1936. pp. 216–217.

1. Anthropology.
2. Geography.
3. Sociology.
4. Economics.
5. Ethics.

6. Ancient history.
7. Medieval history.
8. Modern history.
9. American history.
10. Government.

These social sciences have been arranged in the order of their universality. Modern history should not be limited merely to the European continent, but should include Asia, Africa, and South America as well.

Now if a prospective teacher took merely one course in each of these fields, he would find his college program fairly well filled up; but it is actually necessary to have extensive work in several of these areas. A minimum ideal program would contain:

Anthropology: 1. a general course including reference to prehistoric geology.

Geography: 2. principles of geography, using the western hemisphere, perhaps, for illustrative purposes.
3. the geography of the United States, including geographical influences on our history and our culture.
4. intensive study of the geography of a foreign nation or district.

Sociology: 5. principles of sociology.
6. the sociology of the family.
7. the sociology of selected modern problems.

Economics: 8. the principles of economics.
9. application of economics to our national life, the nature of the course to change from year to year.

Ethics: 10. a course of varied nature; in some colleges the need is met by courses on social ethics, the philosophy of education, the study of the Utopias, surveys of religious movements, or by generalized philosophy.

Ancient history: 11. in this and in all following history courses ample treatment of cultural and economic development is assumed.

Medieval history: 12. with emphasis on Medieval Civilization.

Modern history: 13. Renaissance, Reformation, and Classicism.
14. French Revolution to World War.
15. modern world history.

American history: 16. beginnings.
17. middle period.
18. recent history of the United States.
19. intensive study of a limited field.

Government: 20. government in the United States
21. comparative government.

It should be obvious that such an extensive program, desirable though it may be, is impossible in the average four-year program of teacher preparation. Even if it were, sufficient attention could not be paid any one of the ten general fields. If one desired to be a reasonably well prepared teacher of world history, he would still be forced to take several specialized courses in addition to the ones already listed. If he wished to be well prepared in two fields, economics and sociology for example, he ought properly to take at least six more courses! Thus more than half his total college program would have been prescribed. He would have to pay insufficient attention to his general cultural development, his introduction to education, and his preparation in the other subjects that he might be called upon to teach.

There is no limit to the absurdities that arise when considering this problem abstractly. The field of science is faced by the same dilemma, and for all fields the answer seems to be the same. Let the prospective teacher acquire a broad cultural background and a knowledge of educational practice. Let him spend more than half the total available time on this background and reserve the remaining time for specialization in the field of his special interest.

It is entirely probable that no teacher of the social studies in this country considers himself adequately prepared. There are always other aspects of any problem which would repay study; but it is also probably true that, appreciating his inadequacy, the able social studies teacher does two things: (1) he utilizes his vacations occasionally for further study; (2) he reads as widely as possible in order to fill in the inevitable gaps. Each procedure is recommended for the beginning teacher.

WITH WHAT OTHER FIELDS SHOULD I BE ACQUAINTED?

Successful teachers of the social studies generally have a cultural acquaintance with fields indirectly related to their specialty. The following cultural areas contribute to the social studies:

American literature, with special reference to the literature that reflects the social, political, and economic development of our country.
English literature of a similar nature.
World literature, insofar as it can be had in good translation.
General science, with special emphasis on the impact of modern discovery on thought, knowledge, health, and efficient production.
Music, with special reference to that which can be used as illustrative material in teaching the social studies.

THE BEGINNING TEACHER 11

Art and architecture, both of which can illustrate significantly the social life customarily dealt with in social studies.

Dramatics, including special emphasis on the excellent plays of social
import, and on the moving pictures.

Illustrations from these areas are especially useful when teaching social studies to children with vague or unformed concepts.
Observers of successful teachers usually comment upon the fact
that the fine teacher draws upon a wealth of illustration, especially
when teaching a new idea or when dealing with a far off locale.
In order to acquire a fund of usable material one does not need to
be a scholar in each of the fields identified above. It is probably
sufficient to be acquainted with the general nature of the fields,
selecting from each those elements which will enrich one's teaching.[11]

IS METHOD IMPORTANT IN TEACHING THE SOCIAL STUDIES?

When Judd questioned graduates of teachers colleges, he found
that most of them regretted that they had worked so much on
methods and had spent so little time on content; but when he
questioned graduates of liberal arts colleges, they replied that they
considered themselves adequately prepared in content but very
inadequately in method.[12] Judd's findings could probably be du-
plicated with any group of recent graduates. Teachers soon become
aware of further needs, regardless of their preparation. Those
who are intelligent then proceed to repair the deficiency.

There should be no quarrel between method and content.
Neither is self-sufficient. We have studies showing that very capable teachers with little or no work in the social sciences taught the
social studies better than many teachers who were well prepared
in history and the other subjects.[13] We could conclude from such
evidence that method alone will help a teacher do an average job
of teaching. But it must be remembered that we have no evidence

[11] At present there is no general agreement upon what constitutes adequate
preparation for social studies teachers. The author has reviewed the available literature, but the foregoing discussion represents largely his own opinion, based
upon activity analyses in six schools.

[12] Charles H. Judd, *Preparation of School Personnel*. New York: McGraw-Hill
Book Company, 1938. p. 65.

[13] National Council for the Social Studies, *Eighth Yearbook*. Cambridge, Massachusetts: The secretary, 1937. p. 61; p. 71, items 42–43.

proving that method alone ever produced a great social studies teacher.

Method should be considered as an agency. It permits the teacher to use the social sciences in an attempt to modify the student's attitudes, understandings, and body of accumulated information. Method implies a learner, a teacher, and a thing to be learned. It is the mediating agency that brings these three disparate entities together in what we call education. It is therefore neither prior to nor subservient to subject matter. Method prevents subject matter from becoming tedious and confused; socially useful content prevents method from becoming a tricky, sterile game.

We can formulate the following generalizations concerning method:

1. A teacher's method consists of everything he does in the classroom.
2. Method is also composed of contributory elements that can be isolated, examined, and perfected.
3. Method should be inconspicuous, and not an end in itself.
4. Each teacher's method should be selective and personal.
5. Each teacher's method should grow and become more efficient as progress in teaching takes place.
6. The aim of method is to help the teacher use information and activity to modify student behavior.
7. There is no general "best method," but for any individual teacher there may be a method which is "best" for him.[14]

Generalization number 1 needs further comment. The beginning teacher can clarify his thinking and improve his teaching if he considers method as the combination of all his activities in the classroom. His speech, his approach to a problem, his use of illustrative materials, his skill in making assignments, and his ability to test are all aspects of his individual method. The emphasis he places upon each of the hundred other activities in the classroom is also determined by his distinctive method of teaching. The phrases "unit method" and "contract method" should be reserved for reference to the way in which the teacher arranges his material for teaching. Method is surely greater in scope than the mere arrangement of materials.

Generalization number 4 also needs explanation. It does not mean that since we know nothing of what good teaching is, let each one do as he thinks best. On the contrary, we have isolated

[14] National Council for the Social Studies, *Eighth Yearbook*, p. 63.

many activities that are present in fine teaching. In fact, we have so many excellent procedures at our disposal that no one teacher can hope to use them all. The wise teacher selects from the available procedures those which he can use to the best advantage. He then perfects these to the point where they result in effective teaching. One should neither slavishly follow a formula nor blindly accept each new idea about teaching. The method of the successful teacher never becomes a rigidly crystallized procedure, valuable in itself. All investigators comment on the fact that the good teacher is interested in experimentation.

There are, however, several elements that are present in every successful method. These elements are so generally accepted as necessary for good teaching that they can be listed with little additional comment.

Challenge and interest: good teachers make their work vital. They tend to do this in two general ways. They implement the challenge that is inherent in all social studies work, and they utilize the interests of their students.

Meaningful assignments: when interest has been aroused, the good teacher capitalizes upon it by encouraging the student to study the field of his interest in an orderly way.

Provision for individual differences: good teachers recognize that students vary greatly in ability, interest, maturation, and type of intellect. They try to fit their instruction to the child, so that every student will feel he has some contribution to make.

Help in study: good teachers do not assume that interest in a question is tantamount to the ability to study the question in an effective manner. On the contrary, most good teachers know that even the most brilliant students can be taught to study more effectively.

Provision for activity: good teachers do not lecture to their students day after day. Instead they vary procedures with different types of activity.

Encouragement of clear thinking: good teachers emphasize and extol evidences of rational thinking. Thinking processes can be taught, and effective teachers help their students acquire the habit of rational thought.

Provision for pupil participation: good teachers make their classrooms thrilling places in which students have a chance to participate in arguments, discussions, debates, formal pro-

grams, and informal meetings. This participation should follow careful study and accumulation of evidence.

Evaluation: good teachers are aware that they must test for
more than mere presence of facts. They refer to the objectives of their courses and endeavor to discover the degree of
success they have had in attaining those objectives.

In addition to the common elements of good teaching listed
above, there are several problems peculiar to the social studies.
Insofar as the teacher can solve these problems effectively, his
chances for success in the field are enhanced. It seems essential
that every teacher of the social studies keep the following truths
before him:

1. *Time concepts used in the social studies are unfamiliar to the
   majority of students.* Wesley has demonstrated this fact.
   Even college students were found who were unable to identify
   with general accuracy time concepts. High school students
   thought the phrase "at the beginning of modern times"
   referred to a time varying between the years 1 A.D. and
   1935. The median identification was 1900. In a similar way
   each of 18 commonly used terms of time was identified with
   similarly amazing results. It is safe to say that every teacher
   of the social studies should become an expert in translating
   time into meaningful experiences.[15]

2. *The majority of places referred to in the social studies are unfamiliar to most students.* The author used Wesley's technique
   in obtaining from college and high school students descriptions of Guatemala, Japan, Wisconsin, tropics, desert,
   Montreal. The common conceptions were so grotesque as to
   indicate not only lack of information but the presence of
   misinformation. The teacher who glibly used a phrase like
   "Japan is invading China" with these students might himself have a picture of what he was saying; his students would
   not.

3. *Many concepts used in the social studies are unfamiliar to the
   majority of students.* Such words as economics, social custom,
   franchise, medieval, and totalitarian are probably completely outside the imagination of the average student until

[15] Edgar B. Wesley, *Teaching the Social Studies.* New York: D. C. Heath and
Company, 1937. pp. 408–409.

he has been carefully inducted into an appreciation of these meanings.

4. *Intricate relationships referred to in the social studies are probably unfamiliar to the majority of students.* Such common words as federal, constitution, league, supply and demand, law, taxable, municipal, and divorce need special illustration and comment before they can be used safely with any anticipation that the entire class will accept a common meaning.

The social studies teacher should think of himself as a pilot aiding his students in their journey through a largely unknown world. True, he will find some students with an unusual fund of information, but he will find just as many who comprehend little or nothing of their world and its relationships. It is the teacher's job both to supply the opportunity for acquiring new information and to be the catalytic agency that precipitates present knowledge into meaningful understandings and generalizations. To do so, he must be constantly aware of the four problems identified above.

If anyone doubts the primary importance of dealing with these unknowns of time, place, concept, and interrelationships, let him present the following sentence to a group of average students. "In 1873 the United States hovered on the brink of an economic abyss." He will probably find that his students' conception of 1873 is quite garbled. The United States will not mean quite the same to any two of the students. "Hovering on the brink" is an uncommon expression and one very difficult to understand with any degree of accuracy; and an "economic abyss" is almost incomprehensible unless explained in relationship to actual and potential business conditions. Yet children who have been taught by an excellent social studies teacher can grasp each of these four very difficult concepts. It is reassuring to know that any average teacher can learn to teach any concept used in the social studies if he will merely attend to the task of doing so.

Krey has given a succinct statement of the preferred procedure in teaching for social understandings. The method can be recommended as efficient. The teacher should move through the following sequence: (1) places, concrete objects, and persons; (2) events; (3) simple relationships of time and place; (4) relationships to the material world; (5) relationships among people; and (6) intricate social relationships.[16]

[16] Quoted in Edgar B. Wesley, *op. cit.*, p. 222.

The young teacher should judge all pronouncements concerning method in the light of a widely held belief that the end of method is improved teaching, and the end of teaching is the modification of behavior. It would seem wise, therefore, for the beginning teacher to master the essential steps of good method and become adept in handling the specific problems inherent in social studies teaching. Beyond that he should choose eclectically from among established procedures and techniques.

WHAT SPECIFIC METHODS SHOULD I BE ABLE TO USE?

Good social studies teachers appear to use a variety of methods. There is also evidence to show that students learn more and enjoy their learning more when their teachers use varied methods. It is only natural to expect learning to be more palatable when the meat of study is flavored with the spice of variety; but it is reassuring to discover that in addition to being more palatable, varied methods also make learning more efficient. Wilson phrases our present thought on this problem as follows: "There seems to be at least a rough correlation between pupils' achievements and variety in teaching procedure."[17]

The beginning teacher should become familiar with five or six outstanding methods. He should master two or three. The following methods of teaching the social studies seem to be the most popular and efficient:

1. *Improved textbook method.* A fine textbook used without skill can be practically useless in the social studies. Driving children from page 1 to page 650 without making the work meaningful or challenging has been one of the persistent causes of poor teaching, especially in history and economics. Any of the excellent present-day texts in the social studies can be used by a good teacher with very satisfactory results. Teaching from a single text can be improved by the mastery of the following techniques: unit or problem reorganization, challenging overview, meaningful assignments, provision for individual differences, emphasis on understandings and generalizations, socialized recitations, enriched classroom experiences, and directed study. Most good texts are accompanied by workbooks, which, if properly used, will increase the efficiency of the text. Three recent American histories average nine different types of study helps for each unit. There is no longer any reason to blame the textbook itself for the stupid uses to which some teachers put it.

2. *Unit method.* If the beginning teacher has time to master thoroughly

[17] Howard E. Wilson, *op. cit.*, p. 168.

only one method, he should probably learn how to teach by the unit method. We can say at present that available evidence substantiates the claim that the unit method is at least as good as any other method for teaching the social studies. Its superiority is not established. Students, however, seem to have a noticeable preference for it.[18]

The best current discussion of the method is found in the *Eighth Yearbook* of the National Council for the Social Studies. The evidence for and against the method and its variants is clearly stated there. It is the present writer's opinion that the five-step Morrison procedure of exploration, presentation, assimilation, organization, and recitation is worth the consideration of all social studies teachers. There is less evidence that the teaching-for-mastery technique is worth the unusual effort it demands.

3. *Contract method.* The significant characteristic of this method is that it presents the student with a carefully prepared assignment which he agrees to finish in a given period of time. The method places major emphasis on self-direction, provision for individual differences, and thoroughness in completing a job. An interesting, but not yet validated variant, is to provide contracts on three levels of ability, C, B, and A. The student is free to choose whether or not he will work for a C or for an A. There are obvious objections to this procedure, but research at present available indicates that the contract method may be worthy of careful consideration.[19]

4. *A-U-D Response method.* In this method the student is inducted right at the start into the core of the problem being studied. He is given fifty or sixty generalizations and contentious statements to which he is expected to respond Agree-Uncertain-Disagree. He then scores his responses on a key that indicates the state of his present thinking on five or six large aspects of the problem under discussion. From this beginning, the student launches into a carefully worked out study of the problem, concluding his work with a rigorous evaluation of his information, his skills, and his attitudes. He then checks his growth against the first test he took.

This method has been highly praised by those who have used it. The author has observed its use from the seventh grade through the graduate school. It seems to be an excellent method for teaching work of a problem nature, but not worth the expense of time and effort in a history unit like "The Rise of Jeffersonian Democracy." Perhaps the author has not observed the method used to its best advantage in dealing with such material.

5. *Problem-solving method.* The *Fourteenth Yearbook* of the Department of Superintendence stated emphatically and repeatedly that social studies teachers should consider very carefully the possible merits of problem-solving as a method of teaching. Since that time numer-

---

[18] National Council for the Social Studies, *Eighth Yearbook*. Chapters I and III.
[19] *Ibid.*, p. 54; p. 67 ff., items 7, 33, 35, 37, 46.

ous schools have accepted problem-solving as one of the basic methods. Available evidence, either for or against the method is still meager.[20]

Problem-solving is an attempt to apply present knowledge of thought processes to the procedures of studying social issues. The method is founded on Dewey's statement of how we think. It has been considerably modified by the scientific method of analysis and synthesis. A problem is analysed. Data are collected and applied to the problem. Tentative answers are suggested. They are judged in the light of the available evidence, and conclusions are reached concerning the problem. A final generalization covering a tentative answer to the initial problem is drawn up, and the student's information, skills, and attitudes are carefully evaluated.

Social studies teachers connected with problems courses, sociology courses, individualized work, or contemporary history should investigate the possibilities of problem-solving. The author agrees with the writers of the *Fourteenth Yearbook*. The method has wonderful opportunities in the hands of an alert teacher.

6. *Community Survey method*. The *Ninth Yearbook* of the National Council for the Social Studies is the best available discussion of community surveys as a method of teaching local history, citizenship, and modern social problems. The current emphasis may be merely a fad, or it may be the beginning of a totally new conception of civics courses and problems work. In either event the beginning teacher should be familiar with the possibilities of surveys.[21]

It is obvious that each of the six methods discussed above entails the use of the general elements of good teaching identified previously. In fact, each of the methods is merely a scientific clarification of procedures that have been followed by excellent teachers for years. By investigating current methods and by mastering several of them, the beginning teacher today can share in the procedures that two decades ago were practised only by the exceptional teacher.

WHAT SKILLS AND TECHNIQUES SHOULD I MASTER?

Skills and techniques are the appurtenances of teaching that one uses as peculiar occasion demands. They are constituent parts of any teacher's method, and they are important, for they help the teacher in the routine of his daily work. They have been called

---

[20] National Education Association, Department of Superintendence, *Fourteenth Yearbook*. Washington, D. C.: National Education Association, 1936. Chapter III.

[21] National Council for the Social Studies, *Ninth Yearbook*. Cambridge, Massachusetts: The secretary, 1938.

"the tricks of the trade," but they are more than that. Good techniques are often the basis of a good method.

Techniques used by successful teachers are numerous. The treatment here must be indicative rather than exhaustive. Every teacher acquires little devices which make his work distinctive. Every teacher becomes adept in doing some things better than most of his colleagues. The present discussion concerns the techniques and skills that all teachers should be able to use equally well. First there are the numerous types of classes that occur frequently in social studies teaching:

1. *The developmental lesson:* The teacher, through adroit leadership in discussion, encourages the students to help him plan and prepare the unit of experience to be studied.
2. *The exploratory lesson:* The teacher, through adroit leadership in discussion, discovers how much the class already knows about the problem at hand.
3. *The presentation lesson:* In some types of teaching, teacher-led motivation is necessary. Dramatic presentation of the problem is a good way to accomplish this.
4. *The lecture lesson:* Discouraged in most secondary schools, there are some situations in which the lecture is justifiable.
5. *The question and answer lesson:* The teacher, through well-planned and encouraging questions, develops a well-rounded understanding of a problem with which all the students are more or less familiar.
6. *The discussion plan lesson:* Differs from the preceding lesson mainly in that not all the participating students have studied the same aspects of the common problem.
7. *Socialized lesson:* The teacher is willing to surrender a large part of the leadership of the classroom situation into the hands of the students, who present their findings in one of the various forms of oral presentation.
8. *The directed study lesson:* Class time is given over largely to work on individual projects, whether written, oral, or constructional. The teacher here acts as guide and counsellor.
9. *The lesson with the outside speaker:* A visitor comes into the schoolroom to explain a problem or to defend a point of view. It is assumed that some preparation has been previously made to enable students to appreciate the problem, and that class discussion, either with or without the speaker, will follow.
10. *The field trip lesson:* Students leave the school and observe some aspect of the community in action. The two assumptions of the preceding lesson apply here.
11. *The demonstration lesson:* The class period is devoted to a thorough explanation of, and drill in, some semi-mechanical skill such as using the library or interviewing.

12. *The drill lesson:* The class period is devoted to an intensive drill in some technique such as identifying problems, analyzing sub-problems, mastering correct bibliographical forms.
13. *The review lesson:* The class period is devoted to a review of a large unit of work, generally before formulating a final hypothesis or before taking a test.
14. *The lesson devoted to testing:* Intelligent testing demands an intelligent classroom situation, whether the test is oral, essay, objective, or machine-scored objective.
15. *The lesson devoted to reviewing the test:* Using tests as teaching devices implies that the teacher knows how to conduct a lesson in which the principal material for study is the corrected test taken previously.

In addition to techniques consuming an entire class period there are those more highly specialized ones that can be used incidentally. Most able teachers of the social studies occasionally rely upon the following techniques and skills:

1. *Assignments:* There is an art in making concise, challenging, meaningful assignments. Teachers should vary their assignments, occasionally using teacher-student evolved plans for study.
2. *Identifying individual problems:* Teachers skilled in this technique can meet with a class for half an hour and at the end of the time have most of the students ready to work outside of class upon a problem which has caught their interest.
3. *Explanation:* Giving short, illuminating explanations is essential in the social studies. There are many clever ways of doing this, and every teacher should be accumulating a fund of pertinent explanations.
4. *Illustration:* Some teachers become adept at oral and graphic illustration of involved procedures in geography, history, economics, and government. Cartoons, designs, graphs, and rough maps can be constructed on the board in a moment.
5. *Use of narrative:* Whereas the pure lecture usually bores adolescents, skillfull narrative of unusual information can be a powerful technique. Social studies teachers need to master the art of telling.
6. *Questions and answers:* A recent text for teachers lists more than half a hundred different words with which to start a question. Each word has a slightly different meaning. Each word calls for a distinctive type of thought and recitation.
7. *Use of maps:* Most maps available today are excellent teaching aids. Map companies will gladly send teachers pamphlets explaining how to use maps to the best advantage. One cannot acquire this technique by accident.
8. *Use of cartoons:* The beginning teacher should learn to draw outline cartoons. He should also acquire the habit of using pertinent newspaper cartoons in his classroom. They are good teaching aids.

9. *Use of newspapers:* Large national newspapers have pamphlets advising teachers how to use newspapers in the classroom. The technique is very difficult and rarely mastered. A large percentage of the money spent by social studies departments on newspapers must surely be wasted.
10. *Use of radio:* The technique of using a good radio program is not easily acquired. Teachers should probably not attempt to use the radio unless they have studied the proper techniques for using it.
11. *Use of films:* The teacher should know how to locate, select, project, evaluate, and discuss films for classroom use. This is difficult to do but seems to produce excellent results when well done.

WHAT SHOULD I KNOW ABOUT CHILDREN?

Some very important work in education today concerns our growing knowledge of children. The old idea of an irrevocable Intelligence Quotient has recently been questioned by evidence which shows that environment can change a child's I.Q.[22] We know much more about maturation and the psychology of learning than we did ten years ago. The beginning teacher who does not make an effort to digest this new material is losing a rare opportunity to improve his teaching. Social studies teachers, in particular, need a competent understanding of four aspects of childhood and adolescence.

1. *The beginning teacher should understand the problem of maturation.* An individual child becomes four different people in pre-adolescence, early adolescence, late adolescence and post-adolescence. The fact that these stages in development roughly coincide with the middle grades, junior high school, senior high school, and early college should not delude the teacher into hasty generalizations concerning methods of dealing with students in any one of these school divisions. It is possible to have some students in high school who are pre-adolescent and some who are post-adolescent. The problem of teaching a class consisting of students in such varied stages of development is not the same as teaching a class composed of students who are all at the same point of maturation.

Social studies teachers will probably be called upon more and more to work into their classes discussions of adjustment, guidance, personal relationships, school citizenship, and marriage

[22] George D. Stoddard, "The I.Q.: Its Ups and Downs." *The Educational Record*, Special Supplement, January, 1939.

problems. Teachers who do not know the facts concerning maturation and the emotional changes their students are undergoing will not be prepared to teach such classes.[23]

2. *The beginning teacher must understand normal student interests.* The senior year of social studies is increasingly given over to problems courses. Unless the teacher is aware of normal tendencies, unless he has recently reviewed studies on childhood problems, he will probably be a poor guide for students who otherwise would appreciate a course that deals honestly with their problem. It is probably correct to say that an adult cannot recall accurately his own adolescence, nor can he construct, *a priori*, a course which will meet the needs of present day adolescents. The wise teacher therefore tries to keep in contact with reliable sources of information concerning his students' moral, emotional, economic, social, and intellectual interests. Fortunately, we have today a wealth of reliable information on these problems.[24]

3. *The beginning teacher should understand and appreciate the various types of intelligence.* Intelligence and verbal ability are no longer synonymous. There is ample evidence to prove that individuals have varying kinds of intelligence, of which verbal ability is one of the most important. There is also evidence to show that the social studies have suffered because their appeal has been made primarily to students who could read rapidly and write well. It now seems proper to remind ourselves that other types of students also have a right to profit from courses in the social studies. The beginning teacher can easily learn to distinguish the four following types of intelligence. Seven or eight general types have been isolated at present, but these four seem to include the majority of the school population.[25]

1. *Abstract or verbal intelligence:* the ability to comprehend and manipulate pictures, symbols, abstractions, and ideas. Pupils with high abstract intelligence do well in most secondary school work. In fact, our schools seem to be established solely for such students, yet they number only a small percentage of our total school population.

2. *Social intelligence:* the ability to understand and manipulate people

[23] Daniel A. Prescott, *Emotion and the Educative Process*. Washington, D. C.: The American Council on Education, 1938. Luella Cole, *Psychology of Adolescence*. New York: Farrar and Rinehart, 1937.

[24] Alice V. Keliher, *Life and Growth*. New York: D. Appleton-Century, 1938.

[25] See L. L. Thurstone, *Primary Mental Abilities*. Chicago: University of Chicago Press, 1938.

or the social organizations established by people. Pupils unusually endowed with social intelligence tend to become leaders in school and non-school organizational life. They generally have enough common sense and personal attractiveness to succeed nominally in the average secondary school. They are probably wasting their time, however, in many typical secondary school courses, and in most activities promoted by abstract or verbal-minded teachers.

3. *Mechanical or concrete intelligence:* the ability to understand and manipulate concrete things. The student with high concrete intelligence often excels in practical science, home arts, practical arts, agriculture, and athletics. We can say that such a student, if he has little or no abstract intellectual ability, should not waste his time with many typical secondary school courses. If, however, he is forced to take them, he should be provided with activities adaptable to his peculiar and oftentimes rare ability.

4. *Aesthetic intelligence:* the ability to appreciate experiences in the field of creative art and to manipulate the materials used in the creation of art forms. The student highly gifted with aesthetic intelligence often excels in literature, art, music, home arts, practical arts, and the cultural aspects of other school subjects. Frequently the modern school makes little provision for the education of such students except for art and music classes.

It is obvious that individuals need not be restricted to one of these types of intelligence, but to all outward appearances some people are so restricted. Occasionally a rare individual combines all four types of intelligence to a marked degree.

4. *The beginning teacher should know how to detect and provide for individual differences.* A clear understanding of the characteristics of students will help the teacher provide for individual differences. The current practice in most social studies classes is to teach at the level of the average student. The able student is given more of the same kind of work to do and the slow or retarded student less of the same kind. It is easy to demonstrate that such a procedure is fallacious and even destructive. Studies of brilliant students show that they tend to fail slightly more often than students of only average ability. The cause is obvious. They have no incentive to study.[26]

A rational program for providing for individual differences would give very able students an opportunity to work on advanced intellectual problems. Average students would do much the same kind of work that is now being done in the average social

[26] National Council for the Social Studies, *Eighth Yearbook.* Cambridge, Massachusetts: The secretary, 1937. Chapter IV.

studies classroom; and the very slow student would be participating in activity that was largely non-reading and non-writing in nature. American social studies are postulated on the democratic principle, and it behooves those of us who teach the subjects to pay some allegiance to that principle. Brilliant students have a right to good teaching, and students who are apparently very dull will one day vote and run for office.

Merely suggestive is the following classification of activity according to the type of student to whom it appeals.

1. Activities appealing to and satisfying primarily abstract or verbal intelligence.
   a. Reading for pleasure or for research.
   b. Writing.
   c. Formal arguments.
2. Activities appealing to and satisfying primarily social intelligence.
   a. Informal conversation.
   b. Listening.
   c. Interviewing.
   d. Observing.
3. Activities appealing to and satisfying primarily mechanical or concrete intelligence.
   a. Collecting.
   b. Constructing.
4. Activities appealing to and satisfying primarily aesthetic intelligence.
   a. Drawing.
   b. Painting.
   c. Dramatization.
   d. Music.
   e. Photography.

What Part Does Personality Play in Teaching the Social Studies?

Many studies of teaching identify personality as the most important factor in success. It is difficult to say precisely how important a part personality plays in teaching the social studies. Some investigators conclude that it is the *sine qua non* of good teaching. Entorf writes:

> The ability of an individual to function effectively as a teacher of the family relationship phases of family life education depends more upon her emotional experience than upon her academic training. Therefore, the personal qualities of the teacher of family life courses are much more important than what she knows or what she teaches.

From this point of view, command of content and use of prearranged teaching devices are less useful than is insight into human nature and human relationships.[27]

Steinberg in evaluating the efforts of the New York City secondary schools to provide advanced work for very superior students found that even the ablest adolescents considered the personality of their teachers one of the most important factors. He records the replies of many former students who were evaluating their work after a lapse of ten to fifteen years. A professor of history replied:

> As far as history is concerned, I should say that the order of influence would be: the personality of the teachers, the method of presentation of the subject, the material of the course. If the teacher lacks a dynamic personality, the most inherently interesting subject matter becomes boring.

Another student, now the dean of a school in a New York university, responded:

> Permit me, by repetition, to emphasize that it is my opinion that the personality of great men is of more value in training and encouraging youth than mere knowledge of a subject of skill in presenting the same. Were I to select the staff of a secondary school, I would look beyond degrees and pedagogic ability, and seek out men of character, with a fair knowledge of their subject, who were interested in youth and its possibilities. I would engage men who considered each student as an individual and who delighted in winning the confidence of their charges so that they might plumb their potentialities and encourage them to the fulfillment of their capabilities.[28]

Barr summarizes the research on this problem as follows:

> Notwithstanding the importance attached to discipline, technique, and knowledge of subject matter, it has been found here, as in previous investigations, that the chief sources of weaknesses among poor teachers are defective characteristics of personality.

It should be observed that Barr does not say that the possession of an outstanding personality will lead to inevitable success in teaching. He does say that poor teachers are usually deficient in this attribute.[29]

[27] Mark L. Entorf, "Ends and Means in Teaching Family Relationships," *Parent Education*, April, 1938.

[28] Association of First Assistants in the High Schools of the City of New York, *Educating Superior Children.* New York: The American Book Company, 1935. pp. 129–132.

[29] A. S. Barr, *op. cit.*, p. 117.

On the other hand, there is good evidence to support the belief that the beginning teacher who is content to rely upon personality at the expense of his methods or his content is probably doomed to mediocrity. Smith states categorically in his survey of a hundred excellent social studies teachers that he could find not a single one who relied upon personality alone. He was questioned by Krey on this point.

> Krey: Was there a single instance where the teacher owed her reputation to personality alone outside of her intelligence or quality of work?
> Smith: No, I cannot think of a single instance that would be fairly described by that.[30]

In an analysis of the differences between 1,400 very poor and very good teachers, Bond found that poor teachers generally considered the personality of their college instructors "the most valuable part of college life," whereas teachers who had become known for their unusual ability to teach replied that it was the caliber of their instructor's thought, content, and method that had meant most to them.[31] Bryan found that junior high school students tend to appreciate most their teachers' sympathy and ability to explain but that high school students rate their teachers according to how much the teacher has been able to teach them.[32]

Newer units of work in the social studies call for greater attention to the personality of the man or woman teaching the work. Narrow, morose, pessimistic, maladjusted teachers cannot attain the newer objectives of the social studies; but it seems to the author to be a wretched mistake to assume that possession of a fine personality alone will lead to success.

The statement of an American educator is probably the best summary of the research in this field:

> There are probably not more than one or two teachers in America at whose feet a student should be willing to sit day after day, drinking in only the wonder of the teacher's personality![33]

[30] Edward Payson Smith, *op. cit.*, p. 285.

[31] Jesse A. Bond, *op. cit.*

[32] Roy C. Bryan, *Pupil Rating of Secondary School Teachers*. New York: Teachers College, Columbia University, 1937.

[33] Boyd Bode, lecture to a conference at Ohio State University, July, 1936.

Is It Possible To Develop a Good Teaching Personality?

Assuming that the beginning teacher appreciates the true importance of personality in teaching, it should then be possible to identify a few procedures which will probably lead to a more satisfactory personality. In the first place, the personal gifts of a teacher are judged most critically by the teacher's students. We have evidence that students are among the best judges of teacher personality. What do students deem important in teacher personality? The following traits have been considered significant:

1. *Sympathy.* The teacher is interested in his students. He shows this interest. He is not afraid to have his students know that their problems are important to him. He is especially interested in the future careers of his students.
2. *Understanding.* The teacher knows the basic facts of child and adolescent psychology. He applies this information to each of the situations facing him throughout the day. He is especially apt in dealing with problems of guidance in an objective, yet sympathetic manner.
3. *Helpfulness.* The teacher has a rare gift for explanation, for assisting each student individually, and for aiding each student to master new problems.
4. *Humor.* The teacher is cheerful, happy, good natured, and witty. He can take a joke. He puts students at their ease. He makes his classroom a pleasing, yet efficient place in which to work.
5. *Truth.* The teacher is able to generate a respect for truth. He marks without reference to personal prejudices. He is honest.
6. *Competency.* The teacher is able to teach. His students learn more than in the average class. The work is hard, and yet it is enjoyable. There is a sense of purpose.
7. *Control.* The teacher is able to maintain excellent discipline. He does not raise his voice. He does not lose his temper, yet his students are well behaved.
8. *Appearance.* The teacher is neatly dressed. His hands, face, nails, ears, nose, teeth, and neck are clean. He is free of body odor. His hair is combed.

The beginning teacher should note especially traits 5, 6, and 7. Many teachers begin their careers with the unfortunate misconception that students prize only friendliness and humor. As a matter of fact, all available studies show that students appreciate competency and control. It is true that the more friendly characteristics are usually, but not always, mentioned first. Success in teaching the social studies, however, seems to demand a proper combination of all these traits.

The extent to which an individual can develop these traits is doubtful. Some teachers seem incapable of becoming friendly with their students. Others seem to be unable to develop an attitude of sympathy toward their students. Some are ridiculous in their attempts at humor.

But the social studies teacher is obligated to develop his social traits to their fullest. The social sciences deal largely with the interactions of individuals. The objectives of the social studies deal more and more with the social understandings and accomplishments of the students. It is highly improbable that worthy social behavior can be taught by antisocial teachers. The beginning teacher should take each of the eight traits listed above and analyze the essential contributions of that trait to good social studies teaching. Can a teacher who is unable to understand children help those children understand one another? Can a teacher whose classroom is a madhouse inculcate a love of the democratic procedures? Can a teacher who demonstrates no sympathy for those immediately about him create sympathy for a civilization long dead or a people many miles removed?

Other sections of this volume deal with improving personality. Six specific activities will aid the social studies teacher in this respect: (1) Associate with the social agencies of one's own community. (2) Develop interests outside the school. (3) Participate in a varied and interesting social program with adults one's own age. (4) Read, travel, think, attend plays, see good movies, argue with friends, discuss current affairs, and participate in some creative activity. (5) Learn as much as one can about children. (6) Associate with children in other than purely classroom situations.

Finally, the beginning teacher should see clearly the tragic results of teaching when one is not well adjusted to the very difficult task of dealing year after year with children. Recent investigations of the mental health of teachers indicate that teachers should make constant provision for their own adjustment and social maturation. Many excellent men and women teach until they are sixty-five or beyond, losing little of their wit, force, or competency. They are able to do so largely because they have retained their mental alertness and safeguarded their social adjustments. Healthy teaching personality seems to develop best when it is consciously sought. To varying degrees it is probably within the reach of all teachers.

WHAT STANDARDS SHOULD GOVERN MY PROFESSIONAL BEHAVIOR?

The National Education Association has a clearly defined statement of ethical standards for teachers. Since the social studies deal constantly with moral judgments, it is proper that the social studies teacher should feel obligated to a strict observance of the ethics of his own profession. Other statements of the ethics of teaching have been made in addition to that of the N.E.A. It would probably be wise to study carefully some such elaboration. This chapter can only summarize the principal conclusions governing five areas of relationships.

I. *Relations with students*
   1. Consider every student an individual who has equal rights with other students.
   2. Regard information concerning students as confidential.
   3. Do not tutor pupils in your class for remuneration.
II. *Relations with administrative officers of the school*
   1. Be frank in your discussions with your administrators.
   2. Do not undermine administrative procedures.
   3. Do not discuss problems with a higher administrative authority before first discussing them with your immediate administrative superior.
   4. Be prompt in attending meetings and submitting reports.
III. *Relations with other colleagues*
   1. Do not indulge in gossip at the expense of another teacher.
   2. Help colleagues who are having difficulty, but do not discuss your actions with other teachers.
   3. Leave classrooms neat at the end of every class or every day.
   4. Have records and materials in satisfactory condition for your successor.
   5. Do not apply for a position already held by another teacher.
IV. *Relations with the community*
   1. Extend a courteous welcome to parents and citizens who visit the school.
   2. Do not discuss religious controversies in the classroom.
   3. Assist in community life insofar as possible.
   4. Do not incur long-unpaid debts.
V. *Relations with the profession in general*
   1. Do not seek self-publicity.
   2. Regard contracts as moral obligations.
   3. Do not accept commissions on sales to the school with which you are connected.
   4. Encourage excellent young men and women to enter the profession and discourage those whose prospects are unfavorable.[34]

[34] Adapted from various sources. See especially W. C. Bagley and M. E. Mac-Donald, *Standard Practices in Teaching*. New York: The Macmillan Company, 1932.

WHY DO SOME SOCIAL STUDIES TEACHERS FAIL?

The beginning teacher should now check upon his personal qualifications. He should formulate an estimate concerning his probable success in the field. He should recognize the general causes of failure. The discussion here will be brief. The general causes for teacher-failure have been given in the following order by Knudsen and McAfee in their summary of the evidence.

1. Poor discipline.
2. Poor teaching method.
3. Lack of interest and industry.
4. Poor professional attitudes.
5. Poor personality.
6. Lack of tact or judgment.
7. Lack of cooperativeness.
8. Lack of community and social adjustment.
9. Poor scholarship.
10. Lack of sympathy.
11. Poor health.

The first five are considerably more important than the last six. It is possible that a reinterpretation of the data would place poor personality second on the list.[35] Hart, in his study of students' descriptions of very poor teachers, found these eleven characteristics.

1. Too cross, crabby, grouchy, never smiles, nagging, sarcastic, loses temper, "flies off the handle."
2. Not helpful with school work, does not explain lessons and assignments, not clear, work not planned.
3. Partial, has "pets" or favored students, and "picks on certain pupils."
4. Superior, aloof, haughty, "snooty," overbearing, "does not know you out of class."
5. Mean, unreasonable, "hard boiled," intolerant, ill mannered, too strict, makes life miserable.
6. Unfair in marking and grading, unfair in tests and examinations.
7. Inconsiderate of pupils' feelings, bawls out pupils in the presence of classmates, pupils are afraid and ill at ease and dread class.
8. Not interested in pupils and does not understand them.
9. Unreasonable assignments and home work.
10. Too loose in discipline, no control of class, does not command respect.
11. Does not stick to the subject, brings in too many irrelevant personal matters, talks too much.[36]

It is interesting to note that some of the things poor teachers are blamed for bear a resemblance to things for which good teachers are praised. Good teachers are lauded for "bringing in interesting

[35] C. W. Knudsen and L. O. McAfee, *op. cit.*, p. 226.
[36] Frank W. Hart, *op. cit.*, p. 250.

personal experiences." With poor teachers the same attempt is termed: "brings in too many irrelevant personal matters." This may be explained by a phenomenon that beginning teachers should understand. It is called the "halo" or "aura." If a teacher early establishes himself as unusually good, then even his defects take on a complexion of merit. If a teacher is labeled poor right from the start, than even his better qualities seem affected and unsatisfactory. Experienced teachers know this and work very hard for success, for success in teaching breeds further success.

Insofar as the peculiar problems of the social studies are concerned, we have several descriptions of poor teachers. Harper listed four reasons as to why social studies teachers failed to accomplish their objectives. They were: (1) too much memorization; (2) lack of continuity in the material; (3) dull and uninteresting subject matter; (4) unimportance or uselessness of material.[37] Each of these objections could be overcome by a superior teacher.

Barr found that poor social studies teachers generally: (1) had serious personality deficiencies; (2) were unable to maintain discipline; (3) used poor methods of teaching; (4) or had insufficient command of subject matter. The same author gives a behavior description of a poor teacher.

The typically poor teacher has poor discipline; is incapable of stimulating interest; and makes no provision for individual differences. She follows a textbook assignment and organization of subject matter; provides formal textbook teaching; and makes little effort to socialize class discussions. The poor teacher appraises the pupils' responses but possesses few commentarial remarks for this purpose. She may be lazy; she may loaf or she may bluff; she may nag her pupils, show favoritism, or be too familiar with the boys in her class. Some poor teachers are sarcastic, some dictatorial, and some indifferent.[38]

If the beginning teacher can escape the weaknesses identified above, he should be well on the road to success. There is one important problem still to be discussed, however, before a teacher can claim success.

How Can I Maintain Good Discipline?

Most good teachers will not admit that they ever have discipline problems. Yet poor discipline is the most frequent cause of

[37] Charles A. Harper, "Why Do Children Dislike History?" *Social Education,* October, 1937.

[38] A. S. Barr, *op. cit.,* p. 115.

teaching failure in American schools. It is also the deficiency which will most surely cause dismissal. Buellesfield in 1915, Morrison in 1926, and Knudsen and McAfee in 1936 all report poor discipline as the primary cause of teaching failure.[39]

The beginning teacher should therefore be aware of the problem. In school life as a whole, the following generalizations seem to apply to discipline. Subsequent comment will be made on discipline as it affects the social studies.

1. Good teachers rarely have discipline problems.
2. Poor discipline can usually be attributed to one of three causes: (1) insufficient preparation; (2) poor method; (3) inadequate teaching personality.
3. Any discipline problem can be solved through intelligent application of good teaching practices. This leads to the conclusion that the teacher is usually some way at fault when a discipline problem arises. There are exceptions to this rule, but they are very rare.
4. Good discipline cannot be achieved by sending students out of the room to some higher authority. This leads to the last generalization:
5. Good discipline springs naturally from healthy classroom situations.

Good discipline is especially a concern of the social studies teacher. The newer objectives of the social studies cannot be achieved without excellent, cooperative discipline. In fact, one of the principal objectives of social education should be the generation of behavior patterns which are themselves standards of good discipline. Students must live together as good citizens. Students must be courteous; they must respect the rights of others; they must be self-directive; they must revere the democratic principles; they must become ever more responsible for the successful functioning of their own school and their own classes. Good discipline will help in the attainment of these goals.

A positive procedure is implied in the foregoing statements. Discipline that will lead to an appreciation of the democratic ideals is not going to be strictly authoritarian. The teacher is not going to impose discipline. He is going to establish situations within his classroom which will be productive of good behavior. This does not imply that he will abdicate from his important role

[39] Henry Buellesfield, "Causes of Failure Among Teachers." *Educational Administration and Supervision*, September, 1915. Robert H. Morrison, "An Analysis of the Demands Made in the Employment and Retention of Teachers." Unpublished Master of Arts thesis, Colorado State College of Education, Greeley, Colorado, 1926. C. W. Knudsen and L. O. McAfee, *op. cit.*, p. 228.

THE BEGINNING TEACHER

as the responsible organizer of his classroom. Nor does it imply that he will countenance license or rebellion. It merely means that the successful teacher will create in his classroom a will toward decent behavior. Good social studies teachers encourage the students themselves to become the disciplinarians.

D. V. Smith describes the ideal of constructive discipline in the social studies when he says:

> To attain such discipline the teacher is responsible for:
> 1. Creating learning situations.
> 2. Suggesting activities so material that each pupil will accept some of them as his own, with the feeling that they originated with him.
> 3. Aiding and guiding pupils in their activity work by gentle and indirect methods rather than arbitrary dictation.
> 4. Affording pupils opportunities to use the information which they acquired in pursuing their own distinctive interests.
> 5. Guiding pupils to wider and higher interests whenever they express an activity interest.[40]

The following steps are recommended as a practical approach to the problem of good discipline.

1. Establish yourself immediately as a competent person.
2. Establish standards of deportment on the first day.
3. Introduce change slowly and only after you have proved your ability to teach under any conditions.
4. Remember that until you have disqualified yourself, your students are eager for your friendship and sympathy.
5. Enlist every student in your obvious campaign for decent social behavior in your classroom.
6. As soon as possible, convert your classroom into a semi-political division of the school. Stress laudable citizenship.
7. As soon as possible, introduce informal, social discussion and activity as the principal method to be used in your classroom.
8. Discuss creative, functional discipline with your students as part of almost any social studies course you are teaching. Create group standards which the group will enforce.

If any beginning teacher fears that such a program of gradual progression is too slow, he should remember that only a few very superior individuals can burst into a school and change it over night. If any teacher feels that such discipline takes time and careful planning, he is correct; but he should study the recent findings of Wrightstone, who concludes that such creative discipline actu-

[40] Donnal V. Smith, *Social Learning*. New York: Charles Scribner's Sons, 1937. p. 149.

ally encourages students to learn more than they do under rigidly enforced discipline. Their attitudes, understandings, and mastery of fact all improve when their social studies teachers use the cooperative approach.[41]

A SELF-RATING SCALE FOR SOCIAL STUDIES TEACHERS

Beginning teachers need make no apologies if they are striving for perfection. It has been demonstrated that capable teachers produce better results of all kinds than poor teachers.[42] They help their students and they help themselves. Good teachers are more effective in teaching facts, attitudes, understandings, and behavior. Good teachers are better liked, retain their mental health longer, receive higher salaries, and are more likely to be promoted. The following check list has been devised to help beginning social studies teachers evaluate their strengths and weaknesses. It has been constructed on the basis of the research commented upon in this chapter. The teacher should check each item carefully and formulate a written evaluation of his potentialities in each of the eight large areas. He should restudy this written evaluation from time to time and revise it.

Trait, Ability, or Characteristic	Superior	Medium	Low
I. Is My Personal Philosophy Adequate?			
1. Do I revere truth as the foundation of all social study?			
2. Do I have an intelligent optimism concerning modern life?			
3. Do I believe in the socially useful life?			
4. Am I committed to the democratic way of living?			
5. Have I an alert attitude toward changing trends?			
6. Am I intellectually curious about modern life?			
7. Do I appreciate the cultural contributions of civilization?			
8. Do I participate in some creative or aesthetic experience?			
II. Am I Developing a Personality Suitable for Teaching the Social Studies?			
1. Am I sympathetic in my approach to children?			
2. Do I understand the problems of other people?			
3. Am I helpful to student and colleagues?			
4. Have I a ready sense of humor?			

[41] J. Wayne Wrightstone, *Appraisal of Newer Practices in Selected Schools.* New York: Bureau of Publications, Teachers College, Columbia University, 1935. pp. 75–86.

[42] William H. Lancelot, *The Measurement of Teaching Efficiency.* New York: The Macmillan Company, 1935. p. 66.

THE BEGINNING TEACHER 35

5. Am I a truthful, honest, person?
6. Do students accept my leadership willingly?
7. Am I sincere in my relationships with others?
8. Do I like considerably more people than I dislike?

III. Is My Personal Appearance Satisfactory?
  1. Do I make the best use of my natural appearance?
  2. Do I attend to my clothes as carefully as possible?
  3. Am I always clean? Am I free of offensive odors?
  4. Do I attend carefully to the cleanliness of the following:

Hands	Ears	Teeth
Nails	Nose	Hair
Feet	Face	Neck
	Mouth	

IV. Am I Responding to My Social and Civic Responsibilities?
  1. Am I a well adjusted, well balanced individual?
  2. Do I have a circle of friends outside the school?
  3. Do I adjust easily to new situations?
  4. Do I vote regularly, pay taxes promptly, etc.?
  5. Do I participate in the general civic life of my community?
  6. Do I avoid losing my temper?
  7. Do I avoid sarcasm, fault-finding, petulance, and ill humor?
  8. Can I be a leader without being a dictator?
  9. Can I be a follower without being a carping critic?

V. Have I a Reasonable Command of Subject Matter?
  1. Do I understand and appreciate the meaning of scholarship in the social sciences?
  2. To what extent am I proficient in the following fields:

Anthropology	Economics	Modern history
Geography	Ethics	American history
Sociology	Ancient history	Government
	Medieval history	

  3. To what extent can I use the contributions of the following fields:

American literature	Music
English literature	Art
World literature	Architecture
General science	Dramatics

  4. To what extent am I utilizing the following to increase knowledge and understanding:

Summer school	Movies
Reading	Plays
Research	Music
Travel	Radio

  5. Am I beginning to synthesize the knowledge I have been acquiring?

VI. Are My Methods of Teaching Efficient?
1. Do I work to perfect my method of teaching?
2. Is my classroom a healthy, happy place?
3. Am I able to inspire learning?
4. Do I place sufficient emphasis on attitudes and understandings?
5. To what extent do I understand the following elements of method:

Motivation	Individual differences
Assignment	Thought processes
Activity	Socialized recitations
Directed study	Evaluation

6. To what extent can I minimize the following difficulties:

Time concepts	Vocabulary
Place concepts	Relationships

7. To what extent do I understand the following specific methods:

Textbook	A.U.D. response
Unit	Problem solving
Contract	Community survey

8. To what extent can I use the following types of lessons:

Developmental	Discussion	Demonstration
Exploratory	Socialized	Drill
Presentation	Directed study	Review
Lecture	Speaker	Testing
Question-answer	Field trips	Evaluation

9. To what extent have I mastered the following skills:

Assignment	Explanation	Narrative
Identifying problems	Illustration	Correlation

10. How efficiently can I find and use the following materials:

Maps	Newspapers	Radio
Cartoons	Magazines	Moving picture
Charts	Pamphlets	Current events

11. Do I maintain an efficient democratic system of discipline?
12. Do I attend to the following details of managing my classroom:

Light	Materials
Ventilation	Boards
Cleanliness	Displays

VII. Have I an Ample Understanding of Children?
1. Do I like children?
2. Do children like me?
3. Do I respect the rights and abilities of children?
4. Do I understand how children mature?
5. Have I studied any recent material on student interest?
6. Am I acquainted with modern psychology?

7. Do I recognize and appreciate the following types of intelligence:

Abstract verbal	Mechanical
Social	Aesthetic

8. Can I administer the following types of activity:

Reading	Interviewing	Drawing
Writing	Observing	Painting
Debate	Collecting	Dramatization
Conversation	Constructing	Music
Listening		Photography

9. Am I emotionally stable in my relations with children?

VIII. Is my Professional Conduct Ethical?
1. Do I understand and accept the ethics of my profession?
2. Am I ethical in my relations with my students?
3. Am I helpful and sincere in my relations with the administrative officers?
4. Am I ethical in my relations with my colleagues?
5. Am I ethical in my community relationships?
6. Do I endeavor to improve the ethical standards of my profession?

JAMES A. MICHENER
ON THE SOCIAL STUDIES

Discussion in the Schools

in
Social Education
Volume 4, Number 1, January 1940
Pages 4-5

" During recent weeks a surprising number of school teachers have announced that any teachers detected discussing the war in their classrooms will be in danger of immediate dismissal. These statements are presumably the result of a laudable desire to keep the schools free of hysterical disturbances. Many citizens will sympathize with such a desire, but everyone deeply concerned with the perpetuation of democracy should censure the mistaken steps which have been taken to insure freedom from hysteria. At this time discussion of America's attitude toward the war should not be stifled by the schools. It should be encouraged.

If democracy is forced to jettison its primary principles, there is some question as to whether or not it will have sufficient strength to survive. If its basic tenets are to be killed at their roots in the school, it is probable that democracy is already defunct and that it is publishing its bankruptcy to the world. "

DISCUSSION IN THE SCHOOLS

DURING recent weeks a surprising number of school superintendents have announced that any teachers detected discussing the war in their classrooms will be in danger of immediate dismissal. These statements are presumably the result of a laudable desire to keep the schools free of hysterical disturbances. Many citizens will sympathize with such a desire, but everyone deeply concerned with the perpetuation of democracy should censure the mistaken steps which have been taken to insure freedom from hysteria. At this time discussion of America's attitude toward the war should not be stifled by the schools. It should be encouraged.

American schools have been considered the very bulwark of American democracy. The testimony of great citizens from Thomas Jefferson to Charles Eliot bear testimony to this fact. The schools are at once the primary source and the refreshing spring from which the tenets of democracy obtain life. If free discussion of important problems is proscribed in the schools, a surrender of magnitude has been made.

THE problem may be analyzed in this way. If boys and girls of high school age are to be denied the right of discussing America's part in war, a first principle of democracy has been violated. Government must be founded on the consent of the governed. If war is agreed upon, students who are at present in school will be called upon to help share the burden. They must have a just part in making the decisions that will determine whether or not the country will move toward war.

If one reasons that children of high school age are too immature to share in the problems of democracy, fascism, and communism, he can be answered by the obvious fact that the two latter forms of government urge their youth to participate in all aspects of national life. Democracy must do the same, and the schools must assume leadership in enlisting young people for the cause

of sane government in this country. Secondary school students have amply demonstrated that they possess the mentality and judgment required for the study of national problems.

If it be argued that the question of war is too emotional for study by adolescents, two conclusive answers can be proposed. In the first place, this reasoning is of the "ostrich type." Young people are discussing the war at home. They discuss it wherever any groups gather. They think about it when they read newspapers, when they listen to the radio, and when they go to the moving pictures. Shutting the discussion out of the classroom does not remove an emotionalized problem from the attention of students. It merely drives the discussion into unsupervised centers. In the second place, it is perhaps better for young people to study emotionalized problems in the relative sanity of the classroom than to jump at snap conclusions without the benefit of any thoughtful discussion.

SOME educators have felt that treatment of the war should be excluded from the schools because teachers are not sufficiently informed or stable to teach honestly. If this is true, then American democracy is doomed by its own admission, and repressive measures will not preserve it. Teachers in our schools are representative, responsible citizens. On the whole, they are at least as well qualified by education and study to teach problems of war and peace as the average layman. It is rather obvious that if these favored citizens are not sufficiently intelligent and stable to lead discussions of national policy, there must be millions of voting citizens who are considerably less qualified. This means that there are really only a few supermen capable of making great decisions and that other citizens should delegate all responsibility to these favored few. Accepting such a belief is admitting the sterility of democracy and inviting a regime of dictatorship.

An unlikely explanation of the "gag

rule" may be that a few superintendents feel silence is the safest way to avoid trouble for the school. Acquiescence may be considered a wise administrative step. To such reasoning one can cite history for reply. When the administrators of the educational systems of Rome, medieval Europe, and modern Germany chose acquiescence instead of vitality, they administered the first blows that led to the disruption of their education. In a democracy schools are not built to provide an administrative chessboard on which silent figures are marshalled into interesting but dead patterns. The function of administration is to encourage and make possible the fulfillment of the school's principal obligations.

THROUGHOUT the country today there is probably no topic of more importance for the schools than the open, orderly discussion of America's part in the war. For many reasons this is so. Children of a democracy should be encouraged to participate in the formulation of national policy. If war does come, there will be a long suspension of democratic procedures, and our children need all the experience they can obtain today to fortify themselves against the day when as adults they will be faced with the task of helping to re-establish the ante-bellum democracy. Finally, tax payers have supported the schools for more than a century in the belief that among other things schools trained young people in the democratic way of life. Our schools will be a sorry implementation of that faith if they scuttle to cover at the first threat of difficulty.

If democracy is forced to jettison its primary principles, there is some question as to whether or not it will have sufficient strength to survive. If its basic tenets are to be killed at their roots in the school, it is probable that democracy is already defunct and that it is publishing its bankruptcy to the world.

JAMES A. MICHENER

Harvard University

JAMES A.
MICHENER
ON THE SOCIAL STUDIES

The P.E.A. Report

in
Social Education
Volume 4, Number 8, December 1940
Pages 530-531

" The Commission on Secondary School Curriculum of the Progressive Education Association has presented its recommendations for the social studies.

This reader is forced to consider this volume in the light of the present world confusion. Even though he might like to seclude himself from the radio for a week and contemplate the nature of the social studies as they might exist in a pre-1914 world, he can not do so, principally because the Progressive Education Association for the past decade has been insisting that its members and directors have some special "pipeline to the future." If their contentions have been true, the Association must have restricted its observations to a far distant future; the current statement on the social studies throws very little light on a disturbing present. "

THE P.E.A. REPORT

THE Commission on Secondary School Curriculum of the Progressive Education Association has presented its recommendations for the social studies.[1] The report is well edited, contains extensive bibliographies and an adequate index, and provides much provocative material for consideration. The report follows the now-familiar form of the Commission's previous volumes with an excellent summarizing chapter on the adolescent in American culture, and with individual chapters on the four areas agreed upon by the Association as the organizing points of the curriculum: Immediate Personal-Social Relationships; Social-Civic Relationships; Economic Relationships; and Personal Living. An interesting chapter on evaluation concludes the volume.

In addition to these customary sections, this report contains an appraisal of the current social scene and an interesting chapter on the community. In general, the report is very similar to the Association's *Science in General Education*. It goes far to help round out the statement of the Association's Commission on Secondary School Curriculum. Philosophically, it is an excellent statement and can heartily be commended to all social studies teachers; from the point of view of present day utility, it is a great disappointment.

This reader is forced to consider the volume in the light of the present world confusion. Even though he might like to seclude

himself from the radio for a week end and contemplate the nature of the social studies as they might exist in a pre-1914 world, he can not do so, principally because the Progressive Education Association for the past decade has been insisting that its members and directors had some special "pipe line to the future." If their contentions have been true, the Association must have restricted its observations to a far distant future; the current statement on the social studies throws very little light on a disturbing present.

THE reviewer will be the first to acknowledge that the times are peculiar and that he may be quite unfair in judging the work of this committee in the light of this abnormal present, but he insists that the specific job of the social studies is to provide a chart through just such troubled times. The authors of the report also accept this obligation, for they state: "In these troublous times, the people, with typical American faith in education, have turned to the schools, demanding that the young be better prepared for meeting problems like unto those which have staggered their elders" (p. 1). The people will look in vain to the schools if we have nothing more specific to provide than the substance of this report.

And that is the crux of the argument. Here, in a year of great crisis, one of America's leading educational organizations provides a plan for the social studies, and the plan is vague, confusing, at times contradictory, and generally reticent in offering succinct proposals for procedure. If the Progressive Education Association objects to having its work judged on the basis of expediency, the reviewer will gladly withdraw his strictures and will submit another philosophical review dealing with broad generalities, as does the report itself. But the authors of this were not willing to consider previous social studies analyses in that detached manner. They criticize their most recent predecessors as follows: "The many excellent reports of the Commission on the Social Studies may, indeed, be said to have re-

[1] Commission on Secondary School Curriculum of the Progressive Education Association. *The Social Studies in General Education.* A Report of the Committee on the Function of the Social Studies in General Education. New York: Appleton Century, 1940. Pp. xv, 401. $2.75.

flected, rather than to have resolved, the current confusion in social-studies instruction" (p. 7). The present report goes much further than did the Commission in presenting a workable program, but it, too, "reflects rather than resolves the current confusion."

It reflects the confusion because it will not be specific. One italicized sentence does provide some specificity, and this deserves to be analyzed further: *"It is the function of social studies to use the resources of the social sciences in meeting adolescent needs so as to develop the desirable characteristics of behavior essential to the achievement of democratic values within the realities of the changing American culture"* (p. 23). This is a noble statement of principle; but unfortunately the authors do not go into the actual *how* of developing the "desirable characteristics." When one looks for the *what, when,* and *where* of the curriculum itself the report is frankly deficient. True, the committee which prepared the volume states, "Potentially each type of curriculum organization and each technique of teaching has both virtues and deficiencies" (p. 25). This statement is so broad, so meaningless, that it is hardly worth inserting in a guidebook to desirable practices. Given a nation in political and cultural stress, there must be *some* educational procedures which are better than others. There must be *some* curricular arrangements that are desirable. To deny this is to admit the bankruptcy of American education, and to avoid pointing out these ascertainable areas in the social studies is to compound a delinquency.

THE reviewer is alarmed by the lack of a constructive program (and please don't contend that Chapters IV through VII provide such a program), because he is certain that if educators themselves can not provide such a program, lay, civilian, military, nationalistic, parental, or business groups will. And they will insist upon complete implementation of their programs. The deficiency in the present volume can best be seen in the chapter on social-civic relationships, in which no hint is given of the revolution in these relationships that has been impending for some time past. Conscription, regimentation, labor camps, non-military national service, and the contribution of one's energy to a nationalist endeavor are all ignored, yet the Progressive Education Association itself is at present sponsoring some of these very movements (See *Democratic Education:* Suggestions for Education and National Defense, a Report from the Board of Directors to the Members of the Progressive Education Association, September, 1940, especially areas Three and Four, pp. 11-14).

The present reviewer believes the Association should be courageous and publish a short pamphlet, organized by the members of the Committee that prepared the current report, in which a series of definite proposals is made for the social studies. The schools of the country would welcome such a body of material, and the pamphlet would be a major contribution to present problems; but if the Association thinks it undemocratic to be specific about anything so fragile as the social studies, then the schools will have to look for lay guidance in their problems of social education. If the Association is unwilling to implement the present nebulous report, I am afraid the volume will have to be deferred until pleasanter times as an interesting philosophical discussion, a kind of academic exercise.

JAMES A. MICHENER
Colorado State College of Education
Greeley

JAMES A.
MICHENER
ON THE SOCIAL STUDIES

Teachers in the Community

in

The Social Studies
Volume XXXII, Number 5, May 1941
Pages 219-221

" Last summer Harvard University sponsored a new departure in teacher education. ...[T]he Harvard Graduate School of Education established a program in which secondary school teachers could visit and inspect three New England communities. ...Since it was a first venture, many mistakes were made, but it is safe to say that if the goal of education is the modification of behavior, few courses in teacher education in the country could be rated more highly than this one. No teacher could visit with so many intelligent, willing citizens, young and old, and not conclude that the schools of our country are a much greater social force than he had previously perceived. "

Teachers in the Community

JAMES A. MICHENER

Colorado State College of Education, Greeley, Colorado

Last summer, Harvard University sponsored an important new departure in teacher education. Since teachers are intimately concerned with the social, economic, and political life of their communities, the Harvard Graduate School of Education established a program in which secondary school teachers could visit and inspect three New England communities. Field studies have been common in graduate education, but this particular course had several unique features.

In the first place, it was not strictly speaking a sociological field study; it was instead a sponsored visit of adults into the central operations of a community. The group did not go with microscopes to investigate some small segment of social life. They went as visitors to communities that willingly invited them to look into many aspects of their life. A rare opportunity was afforded to see the school through the eyes of the shoe-worker, the local priest, the unemployed youth, the Y.M.C.A. worker, and the college student who reviewed his education with critical acumen. Business leaders and local officials were unusually helpful, especially in regard to interrogating them concerning their attitudes toward schools.

In the second place, the course was established by educators for educators. Experiences were selected which would "hit home" with teachers. Since it was a first venture, many mistakes were made, but it is safe to say that if the goal of education is the modification of behavior, few courses in teacher education in the country could be rated more highly than this one. No teacher could visit with so many intelligent, willing citizens, young and old, and not conclude that the schools of our country are a much greater social force than he had previously perceived. Even the instructor, who had been over the entire ground once before, was daily surprised at the richness of the experience. Although traversing familiar ground, he had the daily thrill of learning with his students.

He can unqualifiedly recommend such a course for any teacher, or for any teacher of teachers, who is falling into an academic rut.

With the assistance of The Open Road, Inc., a non-profit organization which assists educational institutions in the conducting of field excursions, the Graduate School of Education arranged a plan whereby teachers from the field would enroll in a field study course. The first week was spent in Harvard surveying the general problems. Then the class moved as a body eighty miles away into a very small village in western New Hampshire. Although the group was primarily interested in school and school problems, it endeavored to obtain information indirectly, talking with as few school men in each community as possible. Instead, ministers, farmers, dairymen, creamery operators, school board members, local residents, and young people were met. In many respects this visit was the high spot of the summer, for the group was taken into the midst of a conservative, yet strangely liberal, New England community where it was able to perceive the forces that work upon the schools.

The next visit was to Marlboro, Massachusetts, where the shoe industry has been declining, to the detriment of the town. Here was inspected, as nearly as could be done, the effects of the rise and fall of industrial life upon educational and other institutions. Marlboro, by virtue of vigorous civic pressures, has acquired title to several of the vacated shoe factories and has taken many ingenious steps to recapture a trade that had threatened to depart forever. In Marlboro we were able to meet the men and women who had initiated and supported these efforts. The group was particularly interested in the genesis and operation of a local, incorporated union.

The last visit was into central Maine, where, in the city of Lewiston, the group was able to observe the culminating steps in the transition of that city from a Yankee village, to an Irish town, to a French city. To most of us the knowledge that there were French enclaves in northern United States came as a surprise, if not, indeed, as a genuine shock. In Lewiston the citizens treated us with genuine hospitality. We were able to meet the French leaders and the representatives of the Yankee minority. We were able to study at first hand the very muddled problem of cultural plurality. Especially were we able, through the kindness of the Catholic leaders, to inspect the great problem of certain areas in New England: the transition from a puritan Protestantism to a vigorous Catholicism.

We concluded the course with a final week at Harvard, during which we endeavored to collect and classify our impressions. Apart from the facts collected during the summer, we were all deeply impressed by the willingness of people everywhere to accept us as interested students of a problem in which they, too, were interested. Without exception, every citizen of these communities who agreed to assist us when we were arranging the course, did more than he had originally promised to perform. Ministers brought two guests instead of one; the manager of a creamery not only arranged a luncheon for us, but had the city manager as an unexpected guest to meet us; when a school board met with us, parents of children in school were also invited; and when we went for a visit to an outing club, many of the leaders of the community were there to talk with us. We were not so naïve as to believe that we always received strictly impartial information; quite often we must have been shown the most gleaming side of the mirror, but we were never denied the privilege of inspecting the mirror at our own leisure, holding it in our own hands. At the end of the course we came to the conclusion that most American communities would have received us in somewhat similar manner. Most noticeably, from the point of view of other groups that might wish to initiate some similar program, we were able to meet with young people in every community. We met with them freely, and in most instances we felt that they had talked with us fairly honestly.

CONCLUSIONS

1. Our conclusions concerning life in New England could obviously be only sketchy and quite unscientific. The only one worth noting is that the publicized New England aloofness does not operate in the summer. We could not have been more kindly received anywhere in the country.

2. Regrettably, such courses seem not to attract natives of the district being studied. The people who could have profited most from this course were New Englanders. None joined. It is probable that teachers in St. Louis would not consider taking a course on the realities of community life in St. Louis. Yet it was obvious to all of us that New England citizens wished that their teachers knew more about the community.

3. Although some of the administrative expense of this course was borne by the Progressive Education Association and The Open Road, it seems probable that similar courses could be made to pay their own way or even to show a profit to the institution offering them.

4. Any course like this one would have to be very poor not to awaken teachers from the lethargy into which they too often fall. The simple stories of young people, the obvious faith of older people, and the combined trust of the community in its schools are most affecting things to hear.

5. Teachers throughout the country should hear from children's own lips, and from the reminis-

cences of practically all adults the testimony that the finest thing that ever happens in school is the awakening that takes place when an enthusiastic child comes into contact with a teacher who can inspire him toward some kind of life plan.

6. Teachers should also hear more than fifty per cent of the ablest students, intellectually, admit that they have never come into contact with a teacher who could inspire them toward a life plan. It was almost painful to hear many of these abler students state that they were almost never challenged by the intellectual quality of the work they did in school.

7. We gained the definite, oft-repeated impression that the CCC camps, whatever their defects, were doing a better job with boys in the lower I.Q. ranges than the schools are.

8. We were deeply impressed by the kind of work certain summer camps are doing with ordinary students. By far the most vitally interested youth we met all summer were students in these camps who made it very clear that "here the teachers all stand for some-

thing." Some of us were visibly disturbed by the dilemma of the school being forced farther and farther away from the main job of "standing for something." Spiritual values, wherever we went, were not the problem of the school.

9. It was disturbing to observe the number of young people who gave the impression, sometimes openly stating their wish, that they were casting about for something vital, big, dynamic (a "movement," perhaps) to associate with. Most often the wish was inchoate; at other times it was like talking to German youth in 1931.

10. The job of living together for a summer with other teachers, being forced to share accommodations, is a salutary experience. The instructor definitely feels that he, with each of his students, is a somewhat better teacher because he was forced to subdue his petty interests and caprices for six weeks in order that others might have a better time. A year of such a forced system might grow tedious; an occasional six weeks is a splendid experiment in democracy.

JAMES A.
MICHENER
ON THE SOCIAL STUDIES

The Mature Social Studies Teacher

in
Social Education
Volume 34, Number 8, November 1970
Pages 760-767

" Today I think of myself as a somewhat older social studies teacher, still preoccupied with the same problems that faced me thirty years ago. The only change that I am aware of is that my audience has changed; the subject matter remains the same.

Any young person well grounded in the scholarship of the various fields, who has learned to explore developing problems, and identify likely sore points, and commit himself to their solution, comes away with an insight into our society that prepares him to face recurrent crisis. "

The Mature Social Studies Teacher

by JAMES A. MICHENER

Not so many semesters ago, JAMES A. MICHENER, *nationally-known author of* The Source, Hawaii, *and* Iberia, *was a teacher of social studies and an active member of the National Council for the Social Studies. He has never forgotten—or wanted to forget— that fact. His article, written especially for this 50th Anniversary Issue of* SOCIAL EDUCATION, *makes clear why he states, "I have always thought of myself as a social studies teacher and continue to do so." It is one of the most candid and interesting articles ever published in the journal.*

ONE OF THE BEST THINGS I ever wrote was an article in the Social Studies Yearbook for 1936 in which I explored a subject with which I had had personal experience, the beginning social studies teacher. The article was well received; some of the good things about it suggested to me that perhaps I could one day write professionally.

Today I think of myself as a somewhat older social studies teacher, still preoccupied with the same problems that faced me thirty years ago. The only change that I am aware of is that my audience has changed; the subject matter remains the same.

I tried, in my early days, to be a good social studies teacher but I was never so good as the excellent asso-

760

"Social-studies curriculum-makers must soon decide just how sincerely they believe that their field can contribute to the education of young men and women who in all probability will face and live through a life of rather continuous change."– James A. Michener in *The Future of the Social Studies*, (Curriculum Series: Number One) NCSS, 1939.

ciates with whom I had a chance to work. Howard E. Wilson of Harvard was as fine a man as I was ever to know, and my debt to him so considerable that it could never be repaid. Edgar B. Wesley of Minnesota was the most effective teacher I worked with and whenever I watched his salty, sane approach to life I realized that he possessed a secret and a skill that I would never match. Augustus C. Krey, also of Minnesota, was the most penetrating scholar in our field and it was a privilege to work with him. But the man who gave me the most important personal help was Erling Hunt of Columbia, a shy, taciturn gentleman whom it was never easy to know.

Hunt happened to be the editor of this journal in the years when I was beginning, and also chairman of the editorial board for which I worked. He was an excellent editor with a dry sense of propriety and a lean style. He taught me much about writing, not in personal sessions, for he was an aloof man, but through his total manner. His comment on what I wrote, his precept in what he wrote, his unemotional professionalism all had a deep impact. From him I learned how to put an article together, how to express ideas succinctly, how to keep copy reasonably well cleaned up. My professional debt to him was then and is now considerable, for throughout my adult life I have continued to write social studies.

Any young man who knew both Wilson and Hunt —the former so mercurial and charismatic, the latter so acerb and deflating—realized that he was in the presence of two first-class minds. I learned from each and would have been deprived had I been denied either. Wilson's enormous optimism has colored much of my work; Hunt's hard insistence on clarity has accounted for its type of structure. I could wish beginning teachers no better luck than to encounter in their education two contrasting men like these two, or two great teachers like the gentlemen from Minnesota. As a beginning teacher I was lucky, for I met these men early, worked with them intimately, and profited from almost every experience I had with

them. Without such preceptors I wonder how I would have learned my trade.

Permanent Values

When I started my professional career, the new field of social studies was just coming into being, and when I received my training in the subjects which comprised it I could not have known that I was absorbing material which would have relevance for the rest of my life, but that was the case. I believe that one of the lasting values of social education is that if well organized it does prepare one to grapple with the wild fluctuations of his time.

Any young person well grounded in the scholarship of the various fields, who has learned to explore developing problems, and identify likely sore points, and commit himself to their solution, comes away with an insight into our society that prepares him to face recurrent crisis. Practically everything I learned in my days of exploration from men like Arthur M. Schlesinger, Sr., Kurt Lewin and Louis B. Wirth has been relevant to the large questions which I have had to confront. Time has confirmed the significance of what they foresaw.

Thus, I began to worry about the race problem thirty years ago and nothing that has developed in the interim has surprised me except that fact that the nexus of the problem was to be faced in the north rather than in the south, and even this I should have foreseen had I paid more attention to population shifts. All else has been anticipated.

Similarly, I was informed about the impending crisis of the cities from the first day I started my studies; later I wrote about it and always I have returned to it with fascination. No recent developments in this area have surprised me very much except, as I indicated above, the reluctance of northern cities to act upon the race question.

Wars, depressions, political shifts and the rapid modifications of our moral postures should not have surprised anyone trained in the work of men like Harry Elmer Barnes and Lewis Mumford, and even the hippie movement ought not to startle those familiar with The Children's Crusade or the roving bands that circulated during the Hundred Years' War. I was, however, unprepared for the sudden emergence of drugs as a major problem and I have spent much time recently speculating on what data I ignored which might have warned me of this development.

Because of this background and this continuing interest, I have always thought of myself as a social studies teacher and continue to do so. Not long ago I had the opportunity of serving as secretary to the convention which revised Pennsylvania's constitution; we became the only major state in recent years able to bring forth and adopt a new document, all of our neighbors failed, and I was impressed with the permanence of problems that confront us in government. Each of the difficult areas identified in classrooms forty years ago continues to perplex us, plus new ones that develop with each decade. I found that those delegates who had been well trained in government or law were prepared to grapple with whatever new problems arose, while having at their command the solid groundwork from which they could analyze the recurring problems. Delegates with no philosophical footing were apt to be immobilized by either the new or the old.

Similarly, when I served as president of our Electoral College I found that each of the problems identified by our Founding Fathers as they struggled with the question of how to elect a President continued to have relevance. The dangers they foresaw are more alive today than when they discussed them, and in those dangerous days of early November 1968, when

it looked as if the Nixon-Humphrey contest might wind up in a deadlock, with election being thrown into the House of Representatives, I often referred to the debates of the Constitutional Convention of 1787 and found them strikingly pertinent.

So, as a more mature social studies teacher I find that the field I committed myself to many decades ago is more vital now than it was when I started, more rewarding to those who work in it, more exciting in the challenges it faces, more essential in the help it can provide. I can think of no field that I could have elected which would have been more productive, and every value that I uncovered then is doubly viable now.

Why Did I Quit Teaching?

I was a diligent teacher and with some of my students I found success, for I could get them interested in fields which they had not previously considered. I enjoyed teaching, worked hard to perfect myself, and looked forward to a lifetime of service, which in the normal course of events would now be drawing to its close.

Suddenly, however, I quit the profession. It was not, as some suspected, because the new salary was higher; and it was certainly not because my interest or commitment had in any way diminished. It was with a pang of regret that I left and I have never lost a sense of disappointment in not having stayed with a field I liked so much.

What happened was this. As I was finishing my graduate work at Harvard precisely the kind of position for which I had been preparing myself fell open, almost providentially. I was a little young for the post and could have been rejected on that score, and I knew that at least two of the other professors under consideration were better scholars than I, so I was not foolish enough to think that I either had the inside track or the right to it.

The job went to another man and I was neither hurt nor surprised, but some months later one of the men on the selection committee told me inadvertently that I had never been seriously considered. "Not because of your age. We really wanted a man your age. And not because of your scholarship, because we thought that you might in the years ahead become the best scholar of the bunch. It was because you didn't have a doctor's degree. We had to have that above all else."

Now my education had been irregular, the crucial years having been spent in European universities, and whereas I had degrees that in some ways exceeded the doctorate and an education that certainly did, I lacked the degree itself and was thus ineligible for serious consideration when the top jobs were being filled.

I concluded that if my profession enforced such criteria, I had no future in it and no further interest. When, a few months later, an enticing position was offered me by a large publishing company I accepted automatically and thus left a profession in which I had prospered and which I loved. It was my work in the publishing company that introduced me to the world of books and convinced me that I could find a place in that world.

I wish I could say, as the storyteller ought to, that the man chosen to fill the position I had wanted had turned out to be a much better professor of the teaching of social studies than I would have been. Unfortunately that was not so. Through the succeeding decades I followed his accomplishments with much interest and felt that he wasted the splendid opportunities provided him. His university became no beacon light to illuminate the way of others, no magnet to attract the best young men and women, no proving ground for the preparation of excellent instructors.

Had the attainment of the doctor's degree automatically insured that the recipient would be a superior professor, I think a case could be made in favor of it. In the succeeding decades I have picked up more than a dozen doctor's degrees and I never receive one without a most wry recollection of how poorly this system operated at a crucial period in my life.

I could, I suppose, adopt a sour-grape attitude and claim that my failing to have the degree at a crossroads in my life projected me into a much happier and more productive experience, but that would not be true. I have never ceased to regret my departure from teaching; I have never erased a sense of guilt; I have never felt that what I was doing was other than an extension of my early interest in the social studies and I remain convinced that the writing of books is in no way a better form of life than constructive teaching.

I have always supposed that when I retired I would look around for some small college that could use my background and that I would end my working life as a teacher. In fact, I think of my books as an extension of my early commitments; creative teaching expressed in a different way. Certainly my concern with the social studies—geography, politics, economics, cultural history, current social problems—

has never diminished and I have tried in general to keep abreast of new developments in these fields.

One might say that I was dismissed as a professor but retained as a teacher.

How I Work

I approach each new field as if I were an advanced college senior, or perhaps a graduate student, entering a tough seminar where the competition was to be keen. I stress this because when I write my term paper it is going to be judged by some of the toughest intellects operating, many of whom know more about my subject than I do. Thus, for me education has become always a more exacting process, the requirements more demanding, the final examination even more demanding.

I start my self-imposed seminar by background reading of as profound a type as I can find and handle. I do much more library work now than when I was in college and with a much greater intensity. But the major difference is that since my goals are self-determined and since they can be rigorously delimited —for I work at only one idea at a time—I no longer take notes. I can carry in my head the relevant contents of about five hundred master books and in any one of them I can locate a passage I might want to recover within a few moments, because I can visualize where on the page the sought-for passage occurred and about how far through the book.

I have given so many demonstrations of this capacity that I no longer doubt its accuracy. What I have said, however, applies only if I knew when I read the book that I was going to be interested in such-and-such a topic; if I flagged the topic when I read it, I simply never forget. But if I did not know at the time I read the book that I might later want to refer to an idea which matured later, I am quite powerless to recall where precisely it was that I came upon it. I know that the data resides somewhere among the five hundred books, but I am powerless to find it and only the most lucky kind of reconstruction enables me to recover it. Usually I don't even try, for I have learned that to do so is a waste of time. Of course, when the seminar ends, and the book is written, I cannot recall even the names of the principal sources, so complete does the slate of my mind wipe itself clean.

As one grows older, and his mind better balanced, the book one cherishes is the book which provides generalizations, insights, fresh approaches or oblique and unexpected illuminations. Of the five hundred basic books I refer to in any subject with which I am concerned, I am lucky if I find two or three with this kind of fortuitous insight. Sometimes they are books that the general public holds in little regard; more often they are books which scholars have known favorably for many years and whose reputation has seeped out to the general public. The specific gravity of such works is unbelievably high, sometimes an idea to a page, and much of my intellectual life has been built around them.

When I was writing about Hawaii I found such a book, in which the writer honestly speculated upon what Polynesian life must have been like; a great part of his work was mere guessing, but it was based upon a wide accumulation of fact, and this produced a body of philosophical insight which proved invaluable. The same thing happened when I was working in Israel; among the thousands upon thousands of books written on the subjects I was interested in there was a small book which endeavored to spell out what exactly happened when Greek civilization met Judaism face to face, and the author developed so many brilliant speculations that reading his conclusions was like tossing a bundle of lighted firecrackers from hand to hand.

I do not give the names of these books because to the next reader, without my interest and years of preparatory work, they might prove to be ordinary or even dull. With the developing intellect it is so often a case of coming upon the right book at the right time; if one misses the fortunate moment it cannot be reconstructed and that particular part of one's brain remains undeveloped.

I spend about two years thinking about a book, two years doing background work, two years writing, and whenever I have abbreviated this schedule it has been to my detriment. Since I have published a book every two years, obviously there is an overlap in preparatory work, but I have not been able to do actual writing upon more than one book at a time. I have occasionally halted work on the writing of a major book to complete some lesser job, but this has usually been to my disadvantage and now I try to avoid such interruptions.

I write everything on a typewriter, two fingers at a time and on the slow side. I edit heavily with pen, then retype, then re-edit and retype. People often ask me what the major problem of the writer is and although I rarely tell them, I know the answer: "Saving your eyes." Practically everything I do—original research, drafting the first run-through; editing, retyping, reading galleys—requires eyesight and mine has never been very good. I therefore have to discipline myself strictly; as a result I do not very often read for mere pleasure, a loss which at times seems quite terrible, nor do I look at television as much as most.

It has often occurred to me that if my high school or college had had a perfect counseling system the expert in charge would have told me, "With eyes as poor as yours, Michener, you should not think of research and writing as a career," which would have been sound advice, physiologically speaking, and rather wide of the mark philosophically. I often rewrite up to seven times, never less than three. I have never thought of myself as a good writer, but I am one of the world's great rewriters. I never send out even an important letter in first draft.

Every working hour I am conscious of the fact that I am a trained social-studies scholar. Even the art books which I have published in Asia have stressed the social backgrounds of the artists and I am as deeply involved in the field today as I was when I first started. My reading is in this field; my research is usually upon topics wholly social in origin or largely so. Today the field seems richer than when I started, more rewarding, and certainly more necessary to the good functioning of our society.

Geography: the Queenly Science

The more I work in the social-studies field the more convinced I become that geography is the foundation of all. When I call it the queenly science I do not visualize a bright-eyed young woman recently a princess but rather an elderly, somewhat beat-up dowager, knowing in the ways of power.

When I begin work on a new area—something I have been called upon to do rather frequently in my adult life—I invariably start with the best geography I can find. This takes precedence over everything else, even history, because I need to ground myself in the fundamentals which have governed and in a sense limited human development. (The second book I read is a cultural history, something like Parrington if I can find it, but such books have not yet been written about many parts of the earth, so that frequently I have to do without; in such cases I try the best available history of literature, sometimes with good results.) Most geography books, like most geography courses, are drab affairs and a waste of time. I have dissipated many hours looking at geographies that were not worth the reading, but when you come upon something like Preston James' speculative works on South America the philosophical returns are apt to be high. However, even the poorest regional geography is better than none at all; it at least delimits the field, fixes certain relationships, and drives the reader to a contemplation of his own.

The virtue of the geographical approach is that it forces the reader to relate man to his environment. It forestalls loose generalization founded mainly on good intentions or hope. It gives a solid footing to speculation and it reminds the reader that he is dealing with real human beings who are just as circumscribed as he. Finally, studying the geography of a region like East Africa compels the reader to draw comparisons with Eastern North America.

With the growing emphasis on ecology and related problems of the environment, geography will undoubtedly grow in importance and relevance. I wish that the teaching of it were going to improve commensurately; most of the geography courses I have known were rather poorly taught and repelled the general student like me.

I could make the same wish about geographical writing. It really ought to be much better than it is, with more emphasis upon generalization and philosophical meaning. Television has done much to awaken the general viewer to geographical matters, and many of my neighbors schedule their evenings so that they can watch one or another of the fine color programs featuring the highlights of foreign lands, but this is not what I have in mind when I call for an increase in geographic study. This is merely a pleasant tourism, sightseeing. What is required is the perceptive analysis of the land and man's relation to it. If one has this solid footing, then the television travelogue can be of enormous additional value. Without it, the television program is harmless entertainment and provides little evidence for reaching conclusions on major problems.

I suppose that my books on Hawaii, Israel and Spain have won a rather wide readership primarily because my extended work in the geography of those areas—really minute field work carried on over periods of many years—has provided a solid tactile base for what I had to say. My characters were not drifting in space; they were rooted in the ground. The Hawaiians were in Hawaii and not in some other place, and they were on an island of special construction and not some generalized mainland. Similarly, I could not have written as I did of Israel had it not been for my sustained study, through many decades, of the principle of the Fertile Crescent—purely a geographical concept—and even though I could not accept the thesis that it was this crescent that called

forth much of the history of the area, the thesis and its antithesis were constantly in my mind.

Similarly, one cannot understand Spain without repeated reference to its geographical footing; its peninsula is quite different from Italy's or Scandinavia's and no European nation has been more influenced by its geographical setting than Spain. I was astonished by the reception accorded my book on Spain. I wrote it not for the general public but rather as a kind of reflection by a social-studies teacher who had been pondering certain ideas for a long time. The fact that so many general readers showed themselves to be hungry for such a book, and willing to spend long hours reading it and then writing letters about it, proves I think that there is a need for men trained in geography to explain the significance of other large portions of the world.

I have been asked a hundred times why I do not do the same kind of writing about South America or Africa. The answer is simple. I would love to do such books but I don't know enough. When I write about Asia I have behind me thirty years of reading and travel and speculation. If trouble were to break out in Tibet tomorrow I would be qualified to say something about it for I have been on each of its borders; I know the history of all the nations that surround it; I have read biographies of perhaps a score of men whose lives touched it in the last two hundred years; I understand its religion, its economy, and above all its cultural geography. After a year's intense concentration, I could write fairly intelligently about Tibet, for I would have a large cognitive base on which to draw.

But if the same kind of trouble were to erupt in Paraguay what could I do? I am not familiar with the history of its neighbors, do not know the biographies of famous Brazilians or Argentinians whose lives might have touched Paraguay. I know little of the wars between Paraguay and Bolivia; above all, I know nothing of the cultural geography or the intellectual history of the region. It would take me a good eight or ten years of reading to make myself proficient in this area, and when a man is in his sixties he cannot devote so much time to any project, no matter how much he might wish to do so. When I started to write about Israel, I had behind me a decade of living in Muslim countries, two decades of study of comparative religions, and a lifetime of familiarity with the Bible. Knowledge does not come quickly; competence requires years of investment.

If I were a young man with any talent for expressing myself, and if I wanted to make myself indispensable to my society, I would devote eight or ten years to the real mastery of one of the earth's major regions. I would learn languages, the religions, the customs, the value systems, the history, the nationalisms, and above all the geography, and when that was completed I would be in a position to write about that region, and I would be invaluable to my nation, for I would be the bridge of understanding to the alien culture. We have seen how crucial such bridges can be.

What area would I specialize in? I personally would choose the Arab lands, for we are more in need of understanding there than anywhere else in the world. If I were someone else, I would probably choose Africa, just north and south of the equator, for this region will have enormous impact on American life during the foreseeable future. If I were of a philosophical or religious bent, and especially if I had just written on Spain, I would choose South America, the most misunderstood of our neighbors, the area most deserving of a sympathetic depiction in American letters.

Believe me, if I were well schooled in one of these vital areas and if I had even a modest gift for writing I would have an insurance policy for the rest of my life, because we need perceptive books about these cultures.

The Shameful Period

If my days in the social studies produced great satisfactions, they were responsible also for one of the regrettable segments of my life, one which even now I look back upon with a sense of shame.

In the period of witch hunts sponsored by Senator Joseph McCarthy the axe of suspicion fell heavily upon social studies teachers, or those with similar interests. Because I have throughout my life been constitutionally opposed to joining I luckily entered this era without my name appearing on anyone's blacklist, even though I was more liberal in thought than many of those thus trapped. Also, my last three employers had been *The Reader's Digest,* the *New York Herald Tribune* and the *Saturday Evening Post,* three journals of stable reputation. I was therefore a popular witness for those accused, for my name was known and my record was impeccable, and I was called to give testimony on behalf of numerous friends. In two instances I knew the claimants to have been revolutionaries urging the overthrow of our government and I despised their attempts to weasel out of their former beliefs and to ask my assistance in denying what they had clearly proposed; I refused to testify for them.

For all the others, men and women whose records

were sounder than mine except for their having joined this or that group or having made this or that intemperate statement within the hearing of informers, I testified, sometimes repeatedly and before frightening tribunals. Often my testimony was of no use; prosecutors pointed out that while it was true that I was a writer now, I had been a professor not long previously, and of social studies to boot. But on many occasions what I said helped the innocent to clear themselves, even though, in one instance, we had to fight clear to the Supreme Court, where one of the most damaging character assassins was demonstrated to have been a liar and an inventor out of whole cloth.

How wretched that period was! I could weep when I look back on the wrongs that were done, the foolishness that was enshrined in tribunals. I remember testifying before one such group for two days, going over the same testimony again and again. When a guilty verdict was brought in I was told, "You were one of the most damaging witnesses against your friend." When I asked why, I was told, "Again and again we brought the discussion around to the point where any logical man would have volunteered information about the affair in Alabama, but since you said nothing we could only conclude that you were trying to hide the facts because you too were a participant in them." I had never heard of any Alabama incident, could have said nothing had I wanted to; you see, these trials were held without the accused's ever being told what he was charged with. If I didn't mention Alabama it was not interpreted as proof that I knew nothing of it; it was proof that I was implicated. But no one was allowed to tell me that Alabama was the root problem.

No case of this kind was more disgusting than the charges brought in the state of California against my revered teacher Howard E. Wilson. Because he had spent a spell working for the United Nations, McCarthyite-types waged a strong campaign against him and sought to have him fired from his job at a California university. His defenders were reduced to the ignominy of soliciting from his former students testimonials as to his loyalty. I have found in Twentieth Century history that whenever young people are required to testify as to the legitimacy of older people, something has gone terribly wrong, (Indonesia, Hitler's Germany, pre-war Japan, Stalin's Russia), but when students are asked to give evidence either against or for their professors the whole damned system is rotten and falling apart.

I gave testimony, at Dr. Wilson's urgent personal request. I was told later that it helped him hold onto his job, but I have remained so ashamed of this incident that it scars my memory as if a rusty sword had been drawn across my heart. That was a disgraceful age and to have participated in it in any respect was a lasting shame.

I recall these distasteful matters because the social studies is an area which attracts irresponsible attack, and it will do so in the future. I am much struck these days by the fact that certain powerful critics call both for the abandonment of social studies as a discipline and the solution of those social problems which only the social studies can analyze and solve. The more precarious our position becomes, the more we are needed.

I am particularly impatient with critics from the physical sciences who castigate the social sciences for being less subject to mathematical proof than the physical sciences. The fact that proof is more difficult in the social sciences does not mean that the subject matter being dealt with is less significant; the reasoning should be just the opposite: because the subject matter of the social sciences is so inescapably crucial and so fraught with emotion, systems of attack and proof must be more tentative.

I have said what course I would pursue if I were a young man with writing talent eager to work in the kinds of fields I have worked in. If I were a young man with a political talent—to be used in government, or the management of business, or the law, or the ministry, for example—I would specialize in the humanities, with a strong helping of the social studies, in the sure knowledge that whereas I might have a most difficult time finding a job at age 22, at age 42 I would be among the pool from which this society would be picking its leaders. Government, business, the church, the communicative professions, education will continue to be run by men and women with broad philosophical backgrounds. Scientists will be eligible if after graduation they give themselves the kind of education I am talking about; if they fail they will continue to man the laboratories while men of broad vision run the nation.

The field grows bigger, not smaller. The need for good teachers is greater, not less. My association with it was one of the principal factors of my life and my debt a lasting one.

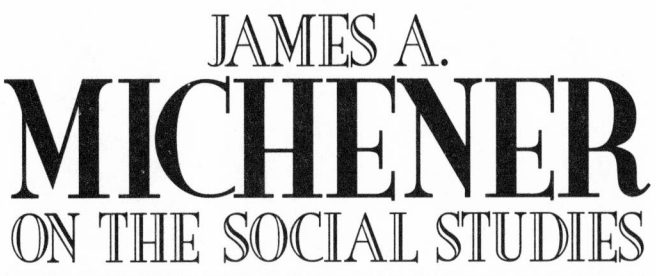

JAMES A. MICHENER
ON THE SOCIAL STUDIES

James Michener Comments on Words and Exploration

in
*Social Education**
Volume 41, Number 5, May 1977
Page 377

❝ I have always believed that an event has not happened until it has passed through the mind of a
creative artist able to explain its significance. I
suppose that is why from the earliest times we have
had the narrators who sat around campfires at
night to recount the heroic adventures of that day.
Because these adventures really did not happen
until they were crystallized into words and comprehensions. ❞

* Comments excerpted from a transcript of a panel
discussion held on July 2, 1976, sponsored by the
National Aeronautics and Space Administration.

James Michener Comments on Words and Exploration

I have always believed that an event has not happened until it has passed through the mind of a creative artist able to explain its significance. I suppose that is why from the earliest times we have had the narrators who sat around campfires at night to recount the heroic adventures of that day. Because those adventures really did not happen until they were crystallized into words and comprehensions.

It is therefore understandable that our first great epic, the Homeric dual poem, dealt primarily with man's earliest adventure in exploring. There is no figure in literature more heroic and permanent than Ulysses. He epitomizes the adventuring characteristic in all of us: the ever searching, the onward probing, the grappling with ancient myths, converting them into present reality, the quest for lands that

JAMES A. MICHENER, author of The Source, Hawaii, Iberia, *and other distinguished works, once was a teacher of social studies and an active member of the National Council for the Social Studies. The following comments were excerpted from a transcript of a panel discussion held on July 2, 1976, sponsored by the National Aeronautics and Space Administration.*

have been mentioned but never seen. It is not by accident that our opening epic deals with the explorer in mankind, because exploring is one of his permanent and attractive characteristics.

I also find the Bible, one of our second or third epics, essentially a story of a tribe motivated by different goals and different gods, moving to explore the area into which they had been called. True, their exploration is as much moral and spiritual as it is physical, but it is always that forward thrusting into Syria, into Egypt, into the Mediterranean, that characterized the second great work.

But it seems to me that if one wants to look at the supreme epic dealing with exploration and come to grips with it, there is no better place to start than the poem of Luiz de Camões, the Portuguese master (usually pronounced Camoëns in English). His great work, *The Lusiads*, extols the explorations done by the men of Lusitania. The poem deals with Vasco da Gama, a man of extraordinary quality, setting out to explore the hidden corners of the world. The book is a paean to the glory of the explorer. It is the noblest statement I know of about

why men go forth and what they accomplish when they do so. But the highlight of the book, and I commend this to you above everything else I will say, comes in Book 4, verses 94 to 104, in which, as the great caravels set forth on this immortal exploration, the old man of Belem appears, sitting by the side of the bay to watch as the ships go down. He utters a most marvelous lament for the insatiable appetite of all who are lured to the horizon. He predicts that this great expedition can come to no good end. The Portuguese will explore new lands but they will give those lands no new light. The ships will go forth but they will not carry any goodness with them to the new lands. The expedition must end in futility and folly, and he continues for 10 wonderful verses, summarizing the arguments that will later be thrown at space exploration: that explorers always take on more problems than they solve.

But at the end, even this old man who is so pessimistic, so against the grain of all Portugal, is forced to concede:

There is no high or fateful enterprise
By fire, steel, flood, heat, cold though it
  may be
That sons of man have ever left
  untried.
Desperate condition, fate unsanctified.

There is no way to halt this exploration. Portugal will not gain from it, but the knowledge of the world will be extended, the implacable onward thrust of mankind will have been continued. So, with the old man's implicit, though grudging, blessing the great enterprise goes forward.

I cherish these 11 verses of Camões because they epitomize the problem of exploration: We never gain as much from it as the wild enthusiasts promise; we invariably gain more than the frightened old men predict. And regardless of predictions, the exploration must go on because it is in man's nature to explore. These verses are a corrective to either kind of excess in talking about exploration, and I particularly must keep them in mind because I have spent the bulk of my life in exploring and have often put my conclusions in writing. ∎

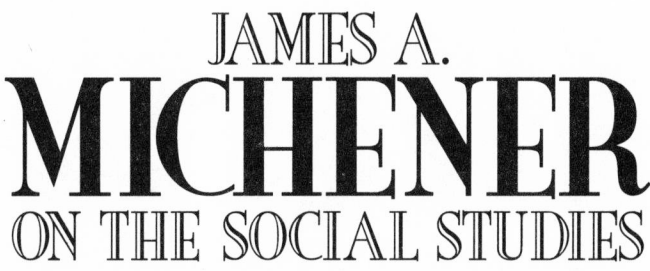

JAMES A. MICHENER ON THE SOCIAL STUDIES

James A. Michener Comments on "The Anti-Science Epidemic"

in
*Social Education**
Volume 44, Number 5, May 1980
Pages 376-380

" All men and women, especially young men and women, ought to feel themselves engaged in an endless war against ignorance, for it is through our defeat of ignorance that we have achieved our great triumphs as human beings.

What we face today, to my amazement, is a phenomenon for which I am not prepared, a counterrevolution against intelligence and especially against science. It disturbs me mightily, even though I am not a scientist and not obligated to the scientific approach.

Our job as educated men and women is to ensure that the scientific approach, which has served us so well, is not dissipated. I do not want to see it rest only in the hands of the highly educated 10 or 15 or 20 percent of scientifically trained people. It must have a broader base than that, or scientists become an elite, off to one side, treasured in moments of crisis, ignored when things are going well, indulged as exotics. "

* A speech delivered at the Washington Conference of the National Space Institute on June 25, 1979.

ideas and issues

James A. Michener Comments on "The Anti-Science Epidemic"

A ll men and women, especially young men and women, ought to feel themselves engaged in an endless war against ignorance, for it is through our defeat of ignorance that we have achieved our great triumphs as human beings. Today the war against ignorance stands in curious posture. We have already defeated the problem of illiteracy—anybody in the world today can be literate. We have eliminated the plague in its many forms. We have assaulted the outer barriers of space. We have even grappled with the simpler forms of mental derangement and maladjustment of the body chemistry. In the conquest of ignorance, we have had tremendous victories.

What we face today, to my amazement, is a phenomenon for which I am not prepared, a counter-revolution against intelligence and especially against science. It disturbs me mightily, even though I am not a scientist and not obligated to the scientific approach.

Perhaps my neutrality entitles me to be more appreciative of the dilemma than I would be if I were deeply involved in it personally. What is sweeping this country and other countries, I fear, is an anti-science movement, a know-nothingism that goes back 200 years, an anti-science hysteria, and the development in politics of an anti-science vote.

This is directly antithetical to the great aims that scientists have had during the centuries. This is a reversal of attitude, and I think we ought to be aware of it. We ought to assess it and, certainly, we ought to combat it.

The Anti-Science Epidemic

Let us consider for a moment what form this anti-

JAMES A. MICHENER, the distinguished novelist, delivered this speech at the Washington Conference of the National Space Institute on June 25, 1979.

science epidemic is taking. On this one brief part of my talk I am perhaps an expert, on nothing else am I; but I have been at the forefront of the anti-science revolution among young people. I have written about it in my novel *The Drifters,* where I was appalled by what was happening to many of our finest and brightest young minds because they were subscribing to this nonsense.

As I worked through the youth movement in those years, I was shocked to find that an enormous number of them were addicted to the I-Ching nonsense, coming out of China, in which it was assumed that a book of recondite material assembled 1,800 years ago was able to produce solutions to current problems.

I was appalled at the number of young people who were taking moral and intellectual and spiritual guidance from the Taro cards. I am today shocked when I turn on a radio station from this community and find that they have on it an astrologer who, when you give your birthdate, tells you what to do for the next five or six years. I was startled at the University of Colorado at Boulder, when I was invited to speak there sometime ago, to check the bulletin boards of the student union and to find not less than nine big expensive advertisements for Indian gurus, each one different and each one with a different doctrine, who were going to explain to the young people of this university the secrets of the universe and how they should reorder their lives. I, who have lived and worked in India, suddenly wondered why, if there is all this intelligence for export, none of it was being applied at home.

I think the young people of Colorado were following very faulty guides indeed, if they felt that they could surrender the whole of the Aristotelian approach to analysis, the whole of the Aquinian approach to morals, the whole of the Thomas Jefferson approach to politics, simply on the word of some guru who applied old falsehoods in a glamorous new light. This seems to

107

be an abdication of reason which I find hard to take. I told the young people, when I met them, that I would stick with the two Thomases, Aquinas and Jefferson, and let them have the gurus.

I have found this rebellion part of a natural rebellion not against science, but against parental authority. They were using scientific aberrations as shock treatment to get the message home to their parents that they were against the whole establishment. And if you're going to be against the whole establishment, what can you do better than throw your whole faith, not in the things that your parents learned at Indiana University or MIT, but in the Taro cards, which will give you a divine insight into things which your parents have completely messed up?

I think that is a large part of it. It is a rebellion against authority, and the most authoritative discipline that the young people come in contact with in their education is the world of science, where certain finite answers are possible.

And this, believe me, is being totally rejected. I think we're going to pay a dreadful price for this. The hopeful thing about it is that this applies only to the general lay public. The education of scientists is going ahead as it always has, and I would suppose the ablest young people I meet today are somewhat better educated than I was at their age. I think they have a brighter promise than I did. So we are dividing our society rather sharply into the elitist group who are at least going through the greater Aristotelian-Socratic approach to learning and that of Immanuel Kant and Jeremy Bentham and other great analysts. The elite is still being educated at a beautiful level, and I am very pleased with that.

It's the great bulk who are forming deviates from that tradition who are going to endanger our political life and the security of our society. This conflict and competition is going to increase rather than diminish. I find a major characteristic of this revolt the runaway fascination that people of ordinary good sense are now expressing in astrology.

I think it's rather shocking the way the media has surrendered to this, so that major newspapers will devote almost a whole page to the addlepated guesses of someone who has given eighty-eight predictions. One turns out to be almost true, and that proves clairvoyance.

In the high school of my home town, they were giving classes for credit in astrology, and it seems to me that this is such an aberration of intellectual leadership that somebody really ought to protect society against it. It is, I think, a reaction to the post-Sputnik age, and it's understandable. All of us who work with ideas are partly culpable, because in the post-Sputnik age science had a pretty clear field. It swept public opinion. It was given a largess and a freedom which it had not had before, and I am not always sure that it used it wisely. It made too many promises; it antagonized teachers in other disciplines, so that some became leaders in the anti-scientific movement.

Science received too much money without public acquiescence or public supervision. It created a mystique to which the ordinary person was not eligible or invited, and against which the ordinary person turned

his or her back. We are now in that period of rejection. Whether this is remediable and reversible, I do not know. I do know that, as someone who is on the firing line myself in these fields, I feel considerable apprehension.

What Do We See Today?

As a consequence of this scientific mood, what do we see today? I come to you as a man somewhat in shock, because I am by nature a scientist, although not so trained. I have never traveled for the last thirty years of my life without a slide rule, in the old days, and now a circular slide rule which I keep in my pocket. I think scientifically and I approach things as scientifically as I can, and what do I find? Trouble.

It seems to me that America's response to Three-Mile Island was about as juvenile and as irresponsible as anything I have ever witnessed. It was hysteria as opposed to studied concern. It was sweeping premature judgment as opposed to calculated analysis and corrective steps. It was economic madness as opposed to cost-effectiveness studies and calculations. It was mob decisions as opposed to the weighing of best alternatives.

I do not see how quasi-scientific economic problems can be settled in that hysterical frame of mind. If such intellectual chaos happened then, it could be repeated in years to come. There is a whole universe of problems in which we are going to have to reevaluate, and recalculate, and reestimate costs and make adjustments in our scale of priorities. If we do so on a hysterical basis, I don't see how an orderly society can move ahead. All of us ought to speak out against that hysterical mode of problem solving.

I find it evident again in our handling of the DC-10. I think this manner of grappling with a problem is about as juvenile as anything I could come up with. It's an abdication of intelligence, it's an abdication of normal problem-solving approaches. It's not a solution at all. It's a reversal of all the great traditions by which we reach our judgments. It is a precise duplication of the Three-Mile Island syndrome. It shows the great need for both political leadership and scientific analysis. I would suppose that one of the contributory faults is that people in charge over the past twenty years have not kept the public conversant with what they were doing. When a tragedy hits, there's apt to be an irrational reaction, because preparation has not been made. This is a sorry strategy for a democracy to adopt for the solution of its complicated problems. . . .

The Factor of Risk

I am especially interested in the moral values involved because I am now working in South African materials and have been doing a great deal of research on the early days of the Cape of Good Hope. Out of every eight or nine ships that passed the Cape of Good Hope in those formative years, the 1500's on, two went down. The cost of linking the great countries of Europe with the equally great countries of Asia was tremendous.

It was not accomplished without vile setbacks, without fears, without apprehensions, without predictions that this could not go on. When one set sail from Amsterdam in the early 1600's to go to Java, one of the great commercial routes of all time, the life expectancy on getting to Java of young men in their very prime of life was a little less than 50 percent. When you went aboard the ship you knew chances were not good that you would ever get there, but the spirit of that period required one to take the risk, and, when enough did, a world of absolute wonder, of enrichment for everyone was attained.

And I think if one looks at Brazil or the Caribbean or the settlement of the United States one finds that same problem, that the cost of getting there was never trivial. It was never 100 percent assured success. It was always an adventure, and those who stayed with the adventure were the ones who sent society forward.

I think that this factor of risk must be kept in mind in the period that we are now involved with. Risk is a fundamental ingredient in scientific advance, whether it be in the abstract sciences, in which I have the greatest interest, or in the applied sciences, like the generation of energy or the development of airplanes. In this adventurous world, there are no securities.

I think that science has been delinquent in creating the impression that there may be. We are now seeing that there are not, and our whole society must be kept informed and instructed on this.

Grappling with Problems

[Another] area in which non-scientific approaches put me in a state of shock is our response to the gasoline shortage. It seems to me that what we have here is the abandonment of leadership, the inability of this nation, with all its computers and all the brilliance of its analysts, to grapple with problems. The inability to tell at any given moment what the supplies of a basic fuel are is, to me, so shocking that I can't come to grips with it.

Had I been director of fuel supplies five years ago, it's quite obvious that the first thing I would have done would be to whip out my circular slide rule and its new improvement—I now work with an HP-25 constantly, and I am through about page 41 of a 181-page manual. I think I have reached my threshold. Anybody who wants the last 100 pages of a good HP manual should see me.

With my calculator I would have said, "Okay, now, what is in the pipeline, what is in the various storage facilities, what are the basic facts?" It would seem to me that any four reasonably intelligent analysts ought to be able to assemble that kind of data and place it on a very secure footing, with an error of plus-or-minus nine.

That is certainly within our capacity. If we have not done it, it can only be because of a malfunction of leadership.

One of the most impressive experiences I have had in my life was in New England many years ago when I wanted to buy a replacement for my car, which had broken down. I was going to get an Oldsmobile. When I went to a dealer—I was then teaching at Harvard and went to a dealer in Cambridge—he had two cars on the floor, and I didn't like either of them. He said, "No problem. Tell me exactly what you want." I did, and it

had about eight characteristics. He said, "Okay, come in Monday, and I'll have it for you."

When I went in, there it was. I was so impressed with such efficiency that I asked him how it had been achieved and he showed me a telegram. He said every Saturday night at 5 o'clock he sent a central clearing house in Boston a coded telegram which [asked] the head office of Oldsmobile in that area where every car within 150 miles was and what its characteristics were. On Sunday he got a cable back telling him where they all were—and for a $20.00 fee he could call another dealer and put a lien on a car, then send his driver over there and get it. On Monday morning he had access to six or seven hundred automobiles. That was my introduction to the fact that management and science working together can organize and do these jobs and can bring rationality into diverse situations.

There's no way that little dealer in Cambridge, by himself, could have supplied my wants. But, with that simple device of exchange of two telegrams, he had the whole strength of the automotive industry behind him. I applaud solutions like that.

In my Naval career, my whole life was turned around, because the Navy had recently adopted a punchcard system, which was very primitive, but did work. As I was completing a very long and arduous tour of duty in the South Pacific, they ran the cards through the punch machine, because they needed somebody who had an MA in history, somebody who had two languages, somebody who had about eight other characteristics—and up came only one card, mine.

Just as I was about to go home, they said, "You know, Michener, we have this wonderful job for you. It will entail two more years, but we think you would be interested because you will have to travel all over the Pacific." It was because of that that I became a writer, so I am a child of the punchcard system.

Swings of Public Opinion

I think that science and people concerned with these applications have been indifferent to the great swings of public opinion, how fast they can happen, with what dazzling speed things can change. I ask all of you to think back four years ago from this day, when our nation was about to make a major decision. How many of you, at that time, even realized that a man like James Carter was in competition for the presidency? It all happened with an overnight swing. There might be today some Republican somewhere, whose name would not come easily to mind to 80 of us, who is in precisely the same situation as Mr. Carter four years ago, with the presidency of the United States right at his fingertips, and we don't even know about it.

I am perhaps more sensitive to those great swings than most, because I deal with them. I wrote a book sometime ago about sports in which I dealt, at some detail, with the great swing that has happened in wrestling. When I was a young man, marvelous, wonderful athletes were wrestling for real—Londos and his crowd—and within three or four years, because of mismanagement and failing to keep the public with them, the whole thing degenerated, and it became a vaudeville show.

I think basketball is in that position right now. It had better make some very, very good decisions, or the public is going to walk away from it. I think we see this in the styling of things for sale; I think we see it in the theatre; we see it in everything; certainly we see it in the field of applied science. If you abandon your intimate relationship with the public, if you fail to keep it with you, you run the grave risk of its walking away from you, the way it walked away from wrestling and the Edsel.

In each of these current problems, space science, as one of our superior intellectual applications, has been delinquent in attending to public relations, by which I mean the keeping of the public in contact with what is happening. Space science has not done a very good job of that, save with the moonshot and, perhaps, the Mars landings.

The pre-disaster preparation in all fields has not been good. Society has been lulled into believing that we have a free ride, and we do not. The quick, solid, masterful decision which may be antithetical to the scientific approach is still one that is forced upon a democratic society. Somehow scientists must participate in that decision-making process to keep the quick decision from being the wrong decision, or even the disastrous decision. Scientists must cultivate harmony and close contact with political leadership and with the leadership of the media.

If one does not do that, I think one loses the ball-game before the whistle blows because then one has no constituency, no support in time of crisis.

We must keep in mind the speed with which these reverses can be made if one loses touch with the political and media leadership. We think we are so secure in church, and education, and IBM, and writers knowing how to create books. It can all vanish overnight. We become the prey to our mistakes more today than we were a hundred years ago, when the decisions could not be reached so rapidly.

Our job as educated men and women is to ensure that the scientific approach, which has served us so well, is not dissipated. I do not want to see it rest only in the hands of the highly educated 10 or 15 or 20 percent of scientifically trained people. It must have a broader base than that, or scientists become an elite, off to one side, treasured in moments of crisis, ignored when things are going well, indulged as exotics.

The general public must be kept abreast of what science is doing and what its potentials are and what its chances for failure are in any given field. The scientific world must do its job better of providing alternatives for the political leadership. The scientific world must, as it has for the past three or four hundred years since Francis Bacon, continue to pursue those goals which history has proved are the soundest bases for the operation of a free society. □

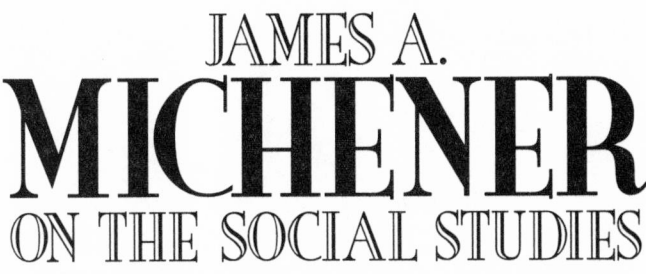

JAMES A. MICHENER
ON THE SOCIAL STUDIES

James A. Michener:
Reaffirmations of a Permanent Liberal

by
Cleta Galvez-Hjornevik

in
Social Education
Volume 51, Number 4, April/May 1987
Pages 250-255

" I think the teaching of geography, which I consider one of the great basic sciences, can help students discover for themselves the great complexity of the earth, its interlocking components, and the manner in which it helps to determine human life.

First of all, the social studies ought to instruct the child and help him or her discover the nature of American political life—the system of checks and balances, federalism, just taxation. The whole structure of American life ought to be understood. The more it's understood, the better.

Students have to know something but maybe it is even more important that they receive from the teacher a sense of enthusiasm about participating in the body politic. I think that is the mark of a good educator. Furthermore, the social studies educator should assist in cultivating, protecting, and advancing society. "

JAMES A. MICHENER:
Reaffirmations of a Permanent Liberal

Cleta Galvez-Hjornevik

James A. Michener's entire career has been devoted to instruction. His novels, essays, and magazine articles have attracted a worldwide audience by promising pleasurable reading and assuring that something of value will be learned. Michener's first career—neglected by his biographers—was as a teacher in schools and universities. As the following biographical sketch by Cleta Galvez-Hjornevik makes clear, it was in the social studies that Michener established his roots in the education profession and developed his writing talent. Our exclusive interview with Michener conducted early last year by Galvez-Hjornevik follows this sketch.

Cleta Galvez-Hjornevik taught high school social studies in Schenectady, New York, from 1976 to 1981, was a Fulbright Scholar in 1978, and received a Ph.D. degree in Curriculum and Instruction from the University of Texas, Austin, in 1984.

While a graduate student at Austin, she became a researcher with O.L. Davis' oral history project that included a planned interview with James Michener. Galvez-Hjornevik uncovered a gold mine of almost untouched information at Harvard and Columbia universities about Michener's early years as an educator and recalls "being carried away by Michener's strong personal identification with social studies during an important period of his life."

She decided then to propose a dissertation topic to her advisor on this aspect of Michener's career. Ultimately, her proposal was approved with the stipulation that she had to be able to get direct and continuing access to Michener himself.

Galvez-Hjornevik has some vivid memories of her first contact with the famous author: "I was screened by the Michener group and eventually met the man himself. He told me he was not enthusiastic about Ph.D. students who take 10 years to write a dissertation. I told him I was sick of being a poor student and wanted to graduate in a reasonable amount of time. We were off and running."

Her dissertation, "James A. Michener: Educator," concentrates on Michener's education career and spans the period from his birth in 1907 until 1941 when he joined the textbook division of the Macmillan Company. The dissertation is under consideration for publication by the Texas A&M University Press.

Galvez-Hjornevik now works on special projects for the 3M Corporation in St. Paul, Minnesota.
—The Editors

James A. Michener began teaching in the 1920s when teaching was viewed as a vehicle for upward mobility and an avenue for continued access to people and books. The most important preparation for teaching school during those years was subject-matter specialization. Michener was well prepared in the subject areas of logic, English, and history.

After graduating from Swarthmore, he was hired as a junior teacher of English at a prestigious private school in Pottstown, Pennsylvania—The Hill School. "The Hill" was a conservative, male, Ivy League, preparatory school, subject to a stringent social milieu—one with which Michener often felt ill at ease.

Operating somewhat outside of the social mainstream, he was drawn to a visionary Quaker, John Lester, who provided him with "teacher training" and exposed him to the ideals of the progressive education movement. Unlike the older, more conservative members of the Hill faculty, Lester understood and advocated the ideals of the progressive education movement, which was gaining momentum in the 1920s and 1930s. Like most young teachers, Michener stayed but one lesson ahead of his students.

After two years, Michener found himself somewhat stifled by the regimen of a Hill School master. In 1931, in the depth of the Depression, he resigned his post to focus again on his own education. He was awarded the Lippincott Fellowship by Swarthmore College, enabling him to study at the University of St. Andrews in Scotland and the University of Siena in Italy. At St. Andrews in particular, Michener matured academically as he read voluminous amounts of European literature.

Progressive Education Association

Though such an event was exceedingly unusual for those Depression years, Michener was contacted in Europe by headmaster George Walton to fill a vacancy in English at the George School—a Quaker, coeducational, progressive institution in Pennsylvania. Michener became immediately immersed in a major, nationwide experiment launched by the Progressive Education Association (PEA)—the Eight Year Study. Exposed to a profoundly different approach toward

113

education, he embraced the principles of PEA and involved himself fully in experimenting with the curriculum.

Michener had an open, mutually supportive relationship with faculty members at the George School whom he described as "the best people in America." His fascination with teaching increased along with his interest in the social sciences. Titillated by the tenuous state of world affairs, he began to teach the social studies.

Involvement in the Eight Year Study afforded Michener a summer with Ralph Tyler and Boyd Bode at Ohio State University, where his interest was again redirected—this time toward the even more progressive laboratory school. He left the George School to take an instructor's position at the College Laboratory School in Greeley, Colorado.

Operated by the Colorado State College of Education, College High School was an experimental school used for preparing undergraduate students to teach. Working as a social studies teacher in a clearly progressive institution appealed greatly to the aspiring educator. They were important years for Michener, during which he received professional attention that would not likely have been available if he had been geographically isolated. Since he had already had considerable teaching experience, he was able to turn his energy to writing and publishing, basing his manuscripts on his timely teaching activities. Being located at a state school of education enabled him to complete an M.A. in Secondary Education. This he did quickly and soon thereafter turned his attention to doctoral study. Michener's experiences in Colorado developed in him a deep concern for public education.

In 1939 Michener became actively involved in the publications committee of the National Council for the Social Studies. As a member and later as chair of this committee, he eagerly used the opportunity it gave him to write. He arranged for publications of contemporary social studies topics and contributed his own manuscripts to NCSS publications. His contributions reflected a strong sense of social consciousness, devotion to progressive education, and unique ability to view a subject holistically. He gained substantial recognition with the publication of *The Future of the Social Studies* (1939).

Lecturer at Harvard

At about the same time Michener was appointed to the NCSS committee, he received a teaching appointment with Howard Wilson at the Harvard University Graduate School of Education. His position as Senior Lecturer allowed him to teach a traditional methods course as well as an experimental course sponsored by the Progressive Education Association. Michener benefited greatly from the stimulating academic atmosphere at Harvard.

Displaying an astonishing amount of energy, he continued to write, teach, pursue his own education as a doctoral student, and edit manuscripts for NCSS. Michener left the hub of the intelligentsia at the end of his term at Harvard and returned to Greeley as an associate professor. This radical change in environment had considerable bearing on his future. His academic responsibilities at Colorado had increased, and he was faced with an impasse in his career.

Although he had completed the course work for the Ed.D. at Harvard, the times required professors in his position to have a Ph.D. in a subject area. Since he did not know either of the required languages, German or French, he knew that a Ph.D. would not be easy to obtain. An offer from Macmillan Publishing Company thus enticed Michener from academia to the world of textbook publishing. After living for years on a teacher's salary, studying in Europe on a shoestring, pocketing a few earnings at Greeley, and receiving a nominal salary at Harvard (though none from NCSS), the stipend offered by Macmillan was very attractive. Less than two years after accepting the Macmillan appointment, however, Michener enlisted in the navy and was plunged into the war in the South Pacific.

The South Pacific years marked the beginning of the career for which James Michener is so well known and admired—a writer of novels and nonfiction. His interest in education and social studies, however, has never waned. In 1970, he wrote "The Mature Social Studies Teacher" for *Social Education*. Now, during the 50th anniversary year of this journal, Michener's provocative thoughts on education and world issues again offer direction for social studies.

Q. *Mr. Michener, let's begin by asking what you regard as important goals for teaching history and geography.*
A. I think the teaching of geography, which I consider one of the great basic sciences, can help students discover for themselves the great complexity of the earth, its interlocking components and the manner in which it helps to determine human life.
Q. *And the teaching of history?*
A. Necessary for a child who is going to have an active life in almost any of the intellectual areas—politics, military, business, universities—is having some understanding of the sequence of civilization, starting with the Chaldeans or the Assyrians, continuing to present-day Uruguay and Peru. I see great good coming from this, and I would allocate a fairly sizable portion of the child's obligatory education to it. History is of crucial importance in the education of a good citizen.
Q. *The title of your proposed dissertation at Harvard was "The Theory of*

> ## "Testing in the social studies is probably the least effective body of testing in the whole school."

Citizenship in Secondary School Social Studies." What can be done through the social studies curriculum to prepare individuals to become good citizens (and by 'good citizens' I mean "socially responsible, civically competent persons")?*
A. First of all, the social studies ought to instruct the child and help him or her discover the nature of American political life—the system of checks and balances, federalism, just taxation. The whole structure of American life ought to be understood. The more it's understood, the better.

Some students will not be able to follow, and I think concessions should be made for them, but anyone who intends to enter intellectual or civic life ought to know that we are different from Britain, Sweden, China, and Russia, and that much of our greatness lies in that difference. Today, I have more respect for the separation of powers than I ever did when I taught it: this is a miraculous concept. Certainly, my faith in the Supreme Court has grown rather than lessened.
Q. *Why do you say that?*
A. The Supreme Court is the way we adjudicate differences between states and social groups, the way we allocate our priorities. The American concept of a supreme court is one of our greatest contributions to international government.
Q. *What role should the social studies teacher play in developing students as good citizens?*
A. Students have to know something, but maybe it is even more important

114

that they receive from the teacher a sense of enthusiasm about participating in the body politic. I think that is the mark of a good educator. Furthermore, the social studies educator should assist in cultivating, protecting, and advancing the society.

Q. *What other institutions have a role in assisting students to become good citizens?*

A. Young people are lucky if they belong to two or three associations outside the school—scouts, 4-H clubs, camps, nature clubs, and also those that pertain to government. In my day, the Young Americans for Freedom (YAF) was a very conservative group for whom I didn't have much sympathy. However, I had enormous respect for what they were doing to bring young people into the political system. The liberals let them get away with the leadership and suffered thereafter.

So, as social studies students, I would call upon the community widely; almost anything one does to introduce oneself into the society of town, city, country, or state would be advantageous. I'm all in favor of that. That's where people get commitment to do better things in their later lives.

Q. *I'd like to change direction a bit. What types of tests or evaluations do you think are most useful in the social studies?*

A. Testing in the social studies is probably the least effective body of testing in the whole school. In science, English, and other subjects, there are tests that do evaluate and predict. But, that's not true in the social studies. History, the awareness of the past, can be tested a little bit perhaps.

Q. *How?*

A. By the normal test procedures: essays, creative projects maybe, construction of units, and factual tests on whether you know what the three branches are, that sort of thing. I'm not a great advocate of chronology testing. In our system, a student ought to know relatively when seven or eight of the great presidents served, such as Washington, Jefferson, Jackson, Lincoln, maybe Cleveland, Theodore Roosevelt, Franklin Roosevelt, and maybe Wilson and Eisenhower.

At the very least, students should know who comes before whom, what the rough sequence is. That's a broad scatter. We're talking about 200 years. One ought to know the experiences of the Revolutionary War in which the nation won its freedom and be able to differentiate them from the Civil War. I would not be very worried if the child didn't know much about the War of 1812 or the Spanish-American War, but

JOHN KINGS

certainly the Revolution, the Civil War, the two world wars—these ought to be imprinted on the student's mind as a structure in which to fit other things.

Q. *Would you suggest anything other than a paper and pencil test?*

A. I think we're talking about two different kinds of pencil and paper tests: One is the multiple choice, for which I still have some respect. I have seen it serve a very useful purpose. The second

---

"I am very apprehensive about what's happening in the United States today. We're in something of a trough in the ups and downs of national life."

---

is the essay test for those students who might be going on. I am very liberal in my thinking that some students really don't need to be ultraproficient in essay-type tests.

If students are entering certain professions, they really don't need to be hot-shot essayists. These students need to know how to read and write; great emphasis should be placed on that. But anyone who is entering any of the even remotely associated learned fields ought to be doing essay tests.

Q. *Social studies is such a difficult subject area because one must know a great deal about many things. What advice would you offer teachers for staying abreast of their subject?*

A. Specialize in two or three things: economics, geography, history, classical history, sociology, or any of the specific

social studies fields to see where our roots came from. Teachers ought to know something in two or three of them—that is, really know who the fine scholars are and what current thinking is.

I would strongly advocate—and I'm suggesting this from personal experience and the experiences of some of my friends—that when you reach the age of 40, you go to a college bookstore and get a good current book in one of the fields you don't know well. The book may be two or three years out of date—buy it secondhand—but read a good geography or an economics text that tries to summarize things.

Then you add one more dimension to your own knowledge, assuming you're keeping up in your own fields. In my life, I've worked with some of the great people of this world in an enormous number of different fields. I am tremendously impressed that most persons I've worked with, at the age of 40 or 50, were educating themselves in something. This is a rule of success in life.

Q. *Your novels teach us much that is interesting and important about the world. What approaches would you recommend for teaching world history to young people?*

A. I am favorably impressed with the elementary school units that presume to project the child into another civilization—the units on ancient Greece, Indian life, Eskimos, or the Congo. The payoff on such studies later in life is enormous. While working in Alaska on my latest novel [*Alaska*, scheduled for publication in September], I had a score of people tell me that they still remember the elementary school unit that they had on Eskimos or life in northern Canada.

The second thing is that either in high school or college one should look at a great period of European or world history in some depth and complexity to see what it was like—the period from the 1790s to the 1830s in Britain, Germany, and France; the great period of the revolution to 1848; the formation of the Greek city-states; or 1914—all these would be very good for that, just to see what was happening in the world.

I stress this with enormous emphasis because that is the way we learn about the complexity and interdependence of a society. At some point, there should be a real digging in to learn something. I always taught that way with, I must say, enormous success.

I used Elizabethan England; I used the period of the civil war both in our country and elsewhere—from 1848 to about 1865—so that you saw turmoil all through the world. If I were teaching now, I would do that even more than I did then. Furthermore, those periods made me dig thoroughly into the collateral cultural evidences of that time—painting, music, opera, architecture.

Q. *As decades pass, one sees changes in the viewpoints and the leanings of the American people. Recently there has been a greater shift to the political Right. Given your background as a social studies teacher, a textbook editor, and an author, how do you perceive this movement?*

A. I am very apprehensive about what's happening in the United States today. We're in something of a trough in the ups and downs of national life. We're losing some of the wonderful attributes that made us strong. The swing to the Right has been far too pronounced in both politics, religion, and newspapers, and somebody ought to blow a warning whistle. So if Teddy White in his similar article proclaimed "Confessions of a Second Look Liberal," you might call mine "The Reaffirmations of a Permanent Liberal."

I will stand by that. I was a good social studies teacher. All the tests I gave and the testimony of my students bear that out. I was good because I always tried to bring my students face to face with their society, where it was going, what its values were, what its dangers were, what was probably going to happen, always speculating and then trying to relate it to the great permanent values of our society. I doubt there were many teachers more patriotically inclined than I was. I also happened to have a very modernist bent and still do. I will never change that. I am willing to look at alternatives.

So, when I look at what's happening today, my first reaction is that the Moral Majority is on to something. They say many good things. They are trying to turn the clock back to a period they prefer, and maybe was better for them at their level. So I don't dismiss the Moral Majority at all. Certainly, their successes in elections—five or six of which I followed carefully—were great. They must have been in harmony with large numbers of the electorate. But when they try to prescribe for me or for my society certain narrow channels of behavior, then I must rebel. The Moral Majority has taken a kick in the teeth, in recent years, when people began to realize what they were doing to our standards and our mores. Most people are pretty much like me—we're willing to listen. When it goes too far, somebody has to blow a whistle.

The fact that the Moral Majority is changing its name and the posture

NEA/JOE DIDIO

under which it presents itself to the American people and then says frankly that they are a political party now is proof that they went through that. Reform movements in the United States flourish for a while and serve a wonderful purpose, but then diminish.

I certainly think that, when I was a young man, the Norris-LaGuardia Act [1932] was needed to set labor free. Everybody, like me, was in favor of Norris-LaGuardia—it would have been incredible not to be. It served its purpose. However, I don't go out beating any drums for Norris-LaGuardia today. The Moral Majority should be seen as another expression of that kind of change in American life. It's all gone far enough—I'm very glad to see people publicly questioning some of its assumptions and activities.

Q. *What do you find especially noteworthy about the changing role of women in U.S. society?*

A. Few people can be more surprised than I at the defeat of the Equal Rights Amendment. I thought it would sail through without any opposition, but the women of the United States seemed not to have wanted it. They may change their minds later . . . and so it goes. There have been tremendous gains, there have been some losses; there's been a good deal of confusion.

The most extraordinary development of all, that doesn't get too much attention, is the change in courtship practices in this country. Young women who are coming of marriageable age and young men of the same age look around in entirely different ways and pick their partners in entirely different ways. And not

MICHENER ON TEACHING

A Chronological List of James A. Michener's Writings on the Social Studies

Compiled by Cleta Galvez-Hjornevik and John Marshall

Michener, James A. "Music and the Social Studies." *Social Studies* 28 (1) (January 1937): 28–30.

Michener, James A. "A Functional Social Studies Program." *Curriculum Journal* 9 (April 1938): 163–64.

Michener, James A. "Sex Education: A Success in Our Social Studies Classes." *Clearing House* 12 (8) (April 1938): 461–65.

Michener, James A. "Bach and Sugar Beets." *Music Educators Journal* 30 (September 1938): 29, 43.

Michener, James A. "Participation in Community Surveys As Social Education." Tenth Yearbook. Cambridge, Massachusetts: National Council for the Social Studies, 1938.

Michener, James A. "The Beginning Teacher." *In-Service Growth of Social Studies Teachers*. Tenth Yearbook. Edited by Burr W. Phillips. Cambridge: National Council for the Social Studies, 1939.

Michener, James Albert, ed. *The Future of the Social Studies: Proposals for an Experimental Social Studies Curriculum*. Cambridge: National Council for the Social Studies, 1940.

Michener, James A. "Discussion in the Schools." *Social Education* 4 (January 1940): 4–5.

Michener, James A. "An Improved Unit Method." *Harvard Educational Review* 10 (March 1940): 211–24.

Michener, James A., and Harold M. Long. *The Unit in the Social Studies*. Cambridge: Harvard Graduate School of Education, 1940.

Michener, James A. "P.E.A. Report." *Social Education* 4 (December 1940): 530–31.

Michener, James A. "Teachers See New England." *Progressive Education* 17 (8) (December 1940): 546–47.

Michener, James A. "Democratic Education." *Social Education* 5 (April 1941): 247–49.

Michener, James A. "Teachers in the Community." *Social Studies* 32 (May 1941): 219–21.

Michener, James A. "Who Is Virgil T. Fry?" *Clearing House* 16 (2) (October 1941): 67–70; published also in *Educational Digest* 7 (November 1941): 4–6; *Clearing House* 19 (October 1944): 69–72; *Clearing House* 23 (September 1948): 12–16; and *Educational Digest* 20 (May 1955): 530–1.

Michener, James A. "What Are We Fighting For?" *Progressive Education* 18 (7) (November 1941): 342–48.

Michener, James A. "Steps in Unit Learning and Teaching." *Eastern Commercial Teacher's Association, Fifteenth Yearbook* (1942), 58–68.

Michener, James A. "Idealism Today." *Education Digest* 15 (4) (December 1949): 44–47.

Michener, James A. "The Perfect Teacher." *Coronet* 30 (June 1951): 21–24.

Michener, James A. "The Mature Social Studies Teacher." *Social Education* 34 (November 1970): 760–67.

Michener, James A. "James A. Michener Comments on 'The Anti-Science Epidemic.' " *Social Education* 44 (May 1980): 376–80. ◻

Cleta Galvez-Hjornevik completed her doctoral dissertation on James A. Michener in 1984, and is now a special projects manager with the 3M Corporation in St. Paul, Minnesota.

John D. Marshall is Assistant Professor of Curriculum and Instruction at the National College of Education, Evanston, Illinois.

with any worse consequence. I'm rather in favor of the radical changes that have taken place in courtship. The end process is still to have a family of one young man and woman who are going to have children and produce the next generation. How you do it admits of many different patterns than the silly rigid one in which I was brought up.

Q. *Have you seen a retrenchment in the area of civil rights under the Reagan administration?*

A. Yes. Generally speaking, under the people that Mr. Reagan has put in charge of civil rights, there has been a retreat. Maybe a better word would be 'standstill'. The courts have not allowed too much of a retreat—I'd rather use 'standstill', a breathing space, a feeling on the part of many people that blacks have enough privileges, and that women, as one of the leaders of the administration said, are not really interested in nuclear warfare or international relations. That sort of thing I find shocking, but it is marking time.

This isn't a total reversal because dedicated liberals like me, many churchmen, and other people in the media, in colleges, and in small towns won't permit it. You can't turn the clock back to the image of the 1830s. It's not going to be permitted.

Q. *What is the role of a "liberal" today?*

A. At a time like this, liberals are very necessary adjuncts to the society to remind people where the no-go line stops. How to protect those rights and fit in with a sharp move to the Right toward conservatism becomes a matter of human tactics. One wants to live one's life, and I don't see any muzzling of the liberal today.

One of the good things so far is that in books you can say almost anything you want to say. You can't do that on television because the time constraints are more prohibitive. But in books and magazines, you can argue all these issues. I've read some absolutely stunning material, often by some conservative writers like Irving Kristol, Teddy

White, or some of my good friends who have turned far more conservative than I. Sometimes they see things far more clearly than I do, and I have to listen carefully when they come up with some new recommendation that I have not thought about yet.

So, I see our society as cautious today, more or less drifting backwards in certain things, somewhat in the trough of a wave. There will be a new surge to take us up to some higher point later on. I have great faith in the American people.

Q. *What are your thoughts about the United States response to apartheid in South Africa?*

A. Well, I spent three years of my life thinking about little but South Africa. I've written a book [*The Covenant*] that is widely used in this field. I felt I have said what I wanted to say in that book, and therefore in recent years I have kept my mouth shut and have not made any statement on apartheid beyond what I made in the book. However, today with Bishop Tutu (a man I admire enormously) and especially Beyers Naude, who is probably the finest man I've met in the last 20 years, if they come here, their heads bloodied by attacks at home and say the time has come when we really ought to apply tougher sanctions against South Africa, I would have to listen.

Q. *How was* The Covenant *received in South Africa?*

A. When I published my book on South Africa in 1980, it was vilified there, it was scorned, it was banned; people made fun of it, attacked me personally, and said that I was a stranger in a strange land and didn't understand anything. I was rather bitter. Later,

---

"Hamilton was an extraordinary man. However, I would hate to live in a society governed by Alexander Hamilton."

---

when they saw that everybody was reading the book, discussing it, and taking opinions from it, they quietly unbanned it because it was circulating anyway.

Q. *What lessons has that experience taught you?*

A. The point is that the creative artist does not serve society well unless he or she is somewhat athwart the society. That should be his or her position and it should be a very honest one: I don't think it should be inflammatory. It should support the people in power and be written with love and affection for the society, never hedging on what view you really see. Then you have the assurance that, 8 or 10 years down the line, people will see that this was about as good a statement as could have been made at the time. I have had that experience three times in my life—total rejection and even public banning; it was illegal to have my books. And then the whole thing turned around!

Q. *The United States is committed to protecting human rights. Often, however, we support a regime that is anti-Soviet but abuses the human rights of its citizens. How can Americans reconcile this inconsistency?*

A. This is about as tough a question as you can ask an American. We have to have faith in our elected officials and support them, but that does not obligate us to kowtow to all of their decisions. If one feels their decisions are wrong, opposing them is a very honorable thing to do. I have never marched or waved

flags, but I have tried to give an honest, undeviating testimony to the great general principles I see governing our nation. That's what a citizen should do.

Some of our recent decisions, such as our reluctance to put pressure on South Africa or our defense of right-wing people everywhere, tarnish the American image somewhat. Therefore, it is more important for those of us who see a larger span of history or a different interpretation of it to say so.

Q. *What might a social studies teacher do when he or she does not agree with a particular point of view embraced by the local community?*

A. I don't know what a teacher, particularly a young teacher, in a community totally committed to a point of view ought to do. I was never reticent. I was lucky. I was always upwardly mobile and felt that, if I didn't work here, I could always work somewhere else. But, that's not true with everybody. I think the first responsibility of a teacher is to hold a job and remain in contact with young people. You achieve your goals through them, not through yourself.

I would make some concessions in order to hold on to a job. However, if those of the extreme Right began to ban all the textbooks I wanted to use, insisted that I eliminate Charles Darwin from the English language, and taught that we can solve our problems with enough nuclear bombs, then I'd just have to break ranks. I think the integrity of a book that gives a true account of Alexander Hamilton and Jefferson, the Civil War, and Vietnam is so precious that it ought not to be perverted by anybody.

I was always a great champion of Jefferson. I still am. I would hope that I mold my life somewhat in his image because he's as good as they come. I can't tell you how salutary it was to read about the party battles of Jefferson with Hamilton and see how often Hamilton was right and Jefferson was wrong on actual techniques of government and money management. Hamilton was an extraordinary man. However, I would hate to live in a society governed by Alexander Hamilton. I would not come off very well.

On the other hand, Jefferson seems not to have been too good an administrator and I'm not sure I'd want to live in a chaotic society governed by Thomas Jefferson. Well, you learn this only through the books and study of the social studies. That's what you want to impart to your children. You can't indoctrinate them, they won't take it, or they'll laugh about it later. But you can inculcate a love of the truth. ❏

Books by James A. Michener

Tales of the South Pacific Macmillan,1947
The Fires of Spring .... Random House, 1949
Return to Paradise .... Random House, 1951
The Voice of Asia .... Random House, 1951
The Bridges at Toko-Ri .... Random House, 1953
Sayonara .... Random House, 1954
The Bridge at Andau .... Random House, 1957
Selected Writings .... Random House, 1957
Rascals in Paradise (with A. Grove Day) .... Random House, 1957
Hawaii .... Random House, 1959
Report of the County Chairman .... Random House, 1961
Caravans .... Random House, 1963
The Source .... Random House, 1965
Iberia .... Random House, 1968
Presidential Lottery .... Random House, 1969
The Quality of Life .... Lippincot, 1970
Kent State .... Random House, 1971
The Drifters .... Random House, 1971
A Michener Miscellany .... Random House/Rodale, 1973
Centennial .... Random House, 1974
Sports in America .... Random House, 1976
Chesapeake .... Random House, 1978
The Watermen (illustrated version of chapters
    from *Chesapeake*) .... Random House, 1979
The Covenant .... Random House, 1980
Space .... Random House, 1982
Poland .... Random House, 1983
Texas .... Random House, 1985
Legacy .... Random House, 1987
Alaska .... Random House, 1988
Journey .... Random House, 1989
Six Days in Havana with John Kings .... University of Texas Press, 1989
Caribbean .... Random House, 1989
Pilgrimage .... Rodale, 1990
The Eagle and the Raven .... State House Press, 1990
The Novel .... Random House, 1991

Art Books

The Floating World .... Tuttle, 1954
Japanese Prints: From the Early Masters to the Modern .... Tuttle, 1958, 1963
The Hokusai Sketchbooks .... Tuttle, 1958
The Modern Japanese Print: An Appreciation .... Tuttle, 1960
Facing East: A Jack Levine Sketchbook .... Random House, 1970